THE CARDIFF BOOK
Volume 3

THE
CARDIFF BOOK

•

Volume Three

•

STEWART WILLIAMS
1977

© Stewart Williams, Publishers,
Bryn Awel, Buttrills Road,
Barry, South Glamorgan

ISBN 0 900807 26 1

INTRODUCTION

The wide range of subject matter in this third volume of the Cardiff series must surely delight those who, like myself, find a never ending source of interest and pleasure in the colourful history—past and present—of the capital city. Once again my thanks are due to the contributors for their generous co-operation. The work of Mrs Elizabeth Dart, Mr John O'Sullivan and Mr Roy Denning has been published in the previous volumes. Newcomers this time are Mr Bill Barrett, headmaster of Gladstone Primary School, Mr Bob Evans of Hill's Welsh Press agency, Mr M. J. Mace, formerly Deputy County Fire Officer of South Glamorgan and now County Fire Officer of Powys, Mr John Scantlebury of the *South Wales Echo*, Mr Peter Arnold and Mr Clive Pritchard.

The book is very much a team effort and I would like to acknowledge the help and encouragement I have received from Mr G. A. C. Dart, F.L.A., South Glamorgan County Librarian, Mr Geoff Rich, Editor of the *South Wales Echo*, Mr Roy Denning, Mr Chris Brain, Mr Bob Skinner and Mr Mike Pincombe. The photographs, as always, add greatly to the interest and for permission to reproduce them my thanks to Cardiff Central Library, the *Western Mail & South Wales Echo*, National Museum of Wales and Mr Haydn Baynham; thanks also to Mr Robert M. Williams who drew the Ely plan.

STEWART WILLIAMS

Printed in Wales by D. Brown & Sons Ltd., Cowbridge and Bridgend

Sir Launcelot . . .

. . . so legend has it, left Cardiff Castle in a hurry, pursued by the wrath of King Arthur. But today's visitors tend to linger over the castle's 1900 years of history—Roman, Norman, Civil War—and the colourful extravaganza of its early Victorian restoration. Cardiff Castle is a favourite with visitors from many lands. And there is an added attraction—the castle is in the heart of the city with one of the world's greatest civic centres just outside the walls.

For special party rates and bookings contact the Technical Services Department, Hodge House, St Mary Street, Cardiff (31033 Ext. 716).

Cardiff Castle

Cardiff

Home of J.R. Freeman makers of fine cigars

Since the turn of the century when J. R. Freeman and Son brought its factory to Cardiff, the city has been at the heart of the British cigar industry. It was here, in 1919, that the famous Manikin cigars were first produced and today—together with Hamlet also made at Cardiff—they are still among Britain's most popular brands. In 1947 Freeman joined the Gallaher Group of Companies and a period of tremendous expansion

began. The present factory in Penarth Road was opened in 1961 and more recently the headquarters of the Freeman organisation moved from London to Cardiff. With another modern factory at Port Talbot, Freeman can claim to be a Welsh Company—and proud of it!

J R FREEMAN & SON LTD
ESTABLISHED 1839

**The people
of Cardiff have always
had good taste.**

It's
BRAINS
you
want

"Traditional beer, brewed at the Old Brewery since 1713"

Big city hospitality
-on the quiet

Just 4 miles away from the bustling centre of Cardiff – the luxurious modern Post House offers you fine cuisine and every comfort in delightful surroundings.

This is the place to come for splendid lunches and dinners, quick meals when you're in a rush and pleasant drinks. You'll dine in style in our elegant restaurant, choosing from an excellent menu and good wine list. The Buttery is open throughout the day for appetising light fare served fast – and there are two well-stocked bars.

Overnight visitors will find first class accommodation, too. Come in for a Post House welcome any time.

For reservations at the Post House contact the hotel direct or your nearest THF Reservations Office: Cardiff (0222) 371889 Manchester 061-969 6111 London 01-567 3444

The Post House

Pentwyn Road, Pentwyn, Cardiff, South Glamorgan.
Telephone: Cardiff (0222) 750-121

Over 800 hotels worldwide.

 Hotels

I was born on Rat Island

by Bill Barrett

I WAS BORN and bread and buttered on Rat Island —a Cardiff geographical location not known to many folk. Mention Tiger Bay and the world knows what you're talking about—but Rat Island, that's another story. Yet besides Rat Island and Tiger Bay, Cardiff has many ethnic groupings— its Newtown area, tucked away between the East/ West dock and the main railway line, was known as Little Ireland and old and loved St Pauls, now gone but not forgotten, as the Irish Church. Little Athens covered an area around the top end of Bute Road, beyond the Feeder Bridge all within a stone's throw of the red-bricked Greek Church. I have heard it said the name Little Madrid was given to several of the streets off James Street at the bottom end of Cardiff Docks. Here many of the Basque refugees lived who came over when Spain erupted into Civil War. Now many of those streets are gone and the others are a ghost town of empty and hollow houses waiting for someone to either knock them down or rebuild them.

Rat Island is not strictly speaking an island any more. Its eastward side used to be represented by the old Glamorganshire Canal which cut through from the Docks into town and into the green hills of the valleys beyond. Its end, of course, was in Merthyr but nobody told us about that in our schools. In fact the canal was rarely referred to by our teachers. They had other people and places in the world to tell us about like the Eskimos and the teak forests of Burma—for these, after all, were in the school syllabus.

The western side of Rat Island was represented by a grey murky river whose name is given to Welshmen everywhere. It is the Taff, the *River out of Eden* of novelist Jack Jones. The river ran all the way up to town, and where it bellied near Grangetown's Penarth Road Bridge it used to be connected to the canal by two huge timber pools suggesting the northern 'border' of the island.

This was our world. Immediately its smell was of mud-flats, new tar bubbling on the streets, oil, fish and drains, but mostly mud-flats. Here was a wonderful play area. The flats dried out to a ripple of cracked surfaces in the long hot summers of our boyhood. For Rat Island like all islands was best in the summer. The canal too had its own smell and a deep fascination which lured us to its side despite parental warnings. My mother would rather give me a copper for the swimming baths in Guildford Crescent than allow me to go in the old canal. We used to walk up Dumballs Road and one day my pal Freddie Dix and I met a boy called Billy Tiley coming down that strangely named road. He expressed amazement that we should be spending good money just for a swim. 'Think' he said, 'what you could buy with a penny and you can have a grand dip in the canal for nothing'. It was a logical argument, and we were easily convinced. We turned back and Billy helped us spend our money on Lucky Bags, treacle toffee and cuttings. The latter were left over odds and ends of sweets, and great value for ½d. We shopped in Lane's that used to be in James Street and later we swam in the cut; a small inlet at the side of the waterway. The canal was dockland's lido. Industry slumbered in the 1930s so there were plenty of ships laid up on its side. These were natural adventure centres and an ideal place to dive from. Some of the modern Olympic swimming stars had nothing on some of the kids I grew up with. They would climb the masts of those ships and stand on the very top, which could not have been more than six or nine inches across, before diving like swallows with scarcely a ripple into the black waters of the canal thirty feet below. Alongside the wharf were mountains of sand where we basked after swimming. After

9

drying out boys would tunnel deep into the sand or slide down on their chests supported by a square of board or corrugated iron. We rarely made it to Barry Island but the canal was fun and it was free.

People in the side streets were sometimes shocked to see a crowd of strange boys steal up the lanes, black from head to foot. These boys had stripped for a swim and after a dive or two had made for the mud-flats near the granite walls which formed the entrance to the canal. Here they would roll in the soft silt until they were as black as a cow's belly. Then armed with branches festooned with any of the flotsam of the tide-line they would march up the streets in threatening order. Smaller children would scream as they approached half in terror and half in excitement. Nearing the canal they would break into a run, screaming like Indians on the warpath before diving into the water to emerge like a shoal of slender white porpoises.

Higher up the canal were moored houseboats of various shapes and sizes. One family in particular stands out in my mind. I believe their name was Sedden. Little was ever seen of the husband for his wife was the real skipper of the craft. Attached to the black gaunt houseboat was a punt. On Sunday afternoon her two sons with caps pulled down over their eyes would row their mother up and down the canal, the distance depending on the humour she was in, and she didn't have much of that commodity. She would constantly scold and shout at them and they always looked frightened to death of her. She carried a walking stick on these cruises occasionally cracking it across their knuckles if they slowed down. All the stuffing seemed knocked out of both of them from early childhood and they never dared to play, even on their way to and from school. Mrs Sedden wore a man's cap and smoked a clay pipe and would sit for hours on deck watching the world go by. She could afford to do this for the rest of the family slaved for her, cleaning, cooking, scrubbing, polishing, carrying water and doing the shopping.

Once when we were playing a street football match on Hunter's Field two forlorn figures watched us from behind the two pillars of bricks representing goal-posts. When the ball was booted into the street one of them ran to fetch it and accidentally collided with a horse-drawn baker's van which was just moving away. He was badly shaken by the accident but when the baker suggested running them home he was terrified. 'Don't worry sonny, I'll explain to your Mum it was an accident', he said. They both shook their heads and hurried away, one helping his injured brother. They didn't want anyone explaining anything to their mother. She might want to know what they were doing in the vicinity of a football match wasting valuable time having a little enjoyment. I heard that sometime later the browbeaten husband had turned on his bully of a wife and had savagely mauled her with a broom handle. The two sons had stood silently by not lifting a finger until she escaped down the gang-plank to nurse her bloodied and bruised limbs all night in one of the derelict sheds along the canal bank. Presumably Mr Sedden was the man in charge after that.

The canal must have produced some rare swimmers and several names stand out. There was the great Paulo Radmilovic who won an Olympic gold in the British water-polo team and there was also Billy Kimber. It was said that Billy once had an offer to become the screen's first Tarzan but had declined stardom to look after his widowed mother, win Taff swims, play water-polo, then a thriving sport, and run his business as a marine-store dealer. He was a solid gentle man who lived quietly in Pomeroy Street and worshipped at old St Stephen's Church in Mount Stuart Square, as regular as clockwork. He was typical of most Rat Islanders—if they couldn't help you they certainly wouldn't harm you, and Billy helped a lot of people.

At the commencement of one 'bathing' season a columnist in the *South Wales Echo* mentioned several Rat Islanders all of whom had distinguished themselves by pulling people out of the canal when they had got into difficulties. He added the number of lives they had saved, and two of them were on the ninety mark. After the publication of the article there was considerable speculation about which life-saver would be first to reach a century. Both men maintained a careful watch and patrolled the waterway with the vigilance of a revenue officer. Any splash of water would see one of them come running, hopeful of adding to their tally. Everyone was so careful that their figures remained static that summer and the autumn found them disappointed men.

Life-savers weren't always successful and from time to time a life would be lost. If the body didn't surface the police came down to drag for it with grappling irons and if that failed a diver had to be engaged. An old Dockland belief was that if bread or straw were thrown into the water at random it would congregate over the corpse. The canal would be deserted for some days following a drowning but within the week things would be back to normal. My father was a

qualified diver, having been trained with the Cornish Salvage Company, and enjoyed the work so much that he later bought his own diving equipment. As a result he was often called out to search for bodies when all else had failed. He was once called in by the police to search the timber float for a post-office boy who had been seized by cramp when he had gone for a quick dip between his split shift. As he groped along the bottom of the float he saw something strange and ghostly come floating towards him. He put up a hand to protect himself and struck the scantily clothed corpse of a woman who rose straight to the surface. There was a gasp from the big crowd who always assembled to watch such searches. Just afterwards he found the boy trapped under the floating timbers so that summer's night instead of one corpse he had found two. 'There are worse jobs in the world', he used to say about such strange work, 'but not many'. The first corpse was that of a local prostitute—a young girl who met her end suddenly

The author (*top right*) with classmates in the top infant class at St Mary's School, Clarence Road, 1930

and swiftly late on a summer's night, an occupational hazard for anyone engaged in such a calling.

The old Taff swim used to end just by the Clarence Road Bridge and great crowds would assemble at this point. Coming out of the water the swimmers would walk dripping wet down to the *Avondale*, presumably to dry and change. The swimmers used to commence at full-tide on Canton Bridge just by the Castle and swim down to the Clarence Bridge, now replaced but not forgotten. To be good enough to swim in the Taff Race gave people considerable status. Later the race was reorganised and held on Roath Park Lake and somehow a lot of the old magic disappeared.

A couple of the sand boats on the canal belonged to Mr Bowles. When he, with the help of his brother, began his sand and gravel business, finances were meagre and he had to run his business on a shoe-string. As a result he didn't always pay the skippers of his sand-boats the top money to which they were entitled. One of these captains was always threatening not to take the ship out and one particular morning with steam up and the tide right he demanded the salary due to him or else the ship would not sail. Words followed and finally the skipper picked up his bag and left. Mr Bowles had to do some quick thinking. Besides the sand and gravel business the brothers did some haulage work with horses and carts. He called out to one of his men, 'Jack, you've been to sea haven't you? What about taking the boat out for me this morning?'. Jack protested that going to sea as a deck-hand was one thing, but taking over a ship was another. The discussion went on and finally Jack in desperation said he didn't really know the way. 'It's easy', said his boss, 'keep on straight down the canal, through the lock and up the cut. Look out for the buoy on the left, keep on the right-hand side of her, then turn the ship round by Penarth Head making sure there's plenty of water beneath you. Head out for mid-channel, watch out for the Wolves and anchor between the two Holms. When you're sucking sand don't over-

fill her this time and come back the same way as you went in, on the full tide'. Jack listened open-mouthed but he finally went and never did anything else until the time he retired, eventually acquiring the prefix Capt. The Wolves incidentally are a line of rocks lying off Flat Holm, one of the reasons for the lighthouse on the island. The Bowles brothers wharf on the canal came to a sudden end when the canal emptied itself in 1951 following an accident. For a time the business was run from the Docks but now the renamed firm operate from the Grangetown side of the River Taff, the river on which Cardiff was born.

Near the canal and within a stone's throw of the Royal Hamadryad Seaman's Hospital was a small house-boat community. Most of the vessels were old life-boats and were purchased for a sovereign on the Docks and then rowed around to settle in a shallow valley leading up from an old ballast beach on the west side of the canal. A top was added, often built of odd scraps of timber, corrugated iron and covered with canvas thickly tarred over. Water was begged from nearby householders until the Corporation eventually erected a stand-pipe near the site. Toilet facilities were rough and ready and the contents of the buckets serving such purposes 'flushed' on the night tide.

In one of these hulks lived 'Donkey' James and his hard-working wife. In a lean-to shed attached to his residence was the family donkey. Mrs James seemed to collect and chop firewood from dawn to dusk. From time to time she would appear dressed in a skirt which came right down to the ground, man's cap fastened with a hat-pin and a coarse sacking apron. Invariably she pushed a small improvised cart, a large box on wheels filled with bundles of sticks, delivering them to many of the corner shops, which were thick on the ground of Rat Island. They sold these sticks, three bundles for a penny, so she worked on a slender profit margin probably receiving fivepence or sixpence for a cartful. Sometimes 'Donkey' James himself would deliver the sticks trotting around the docks on his cart. In the evenings he

The Taff Swim viewed from Fitzhamon Embankment some time in the late '20s showing a section of the crowd with swimmers and boatmen
Photograph courtesy Western Mail & Echo Ltd

would reappear, the cart transformed with some fluttering union-jacks and carrying some tiny benches. 'Ha'penny a ride', he would bawl, and for this modest sum he would rattle half-a-dozen children halfway around the docks.

Mr W. D. Twomley, who is working on a book about his boyhood in Cardiff, relates a humorous story about 'Donkey' James and his long-suffering animal. After his evening's work he would often leave his donkey and cart outside the 'Big Windsor' while he took a little light refreshment indoors. One evening some local hard knocks took the donkey out of the shafts and pushed them through the railings. They then led the donkey

around on the other side and put him back in between the shafts all ready harnessed. Poor old 'Donkey' James. When he stumbled out of the pub a couple of sheets to the wind he loudly up-braided his donkey for somehow getting himself in such a tangle, no doubt sorely puzzled how his animal had managed to put himself in such an extraordinary position. 'It was enough', he declared, 'to make a man sign the pledge'. He never did any such thing however, and together with his little wife went on working, making a living at anything he could turn his hands to until the little community gradually broke up and were rehoused. I have often wondered how those

13

old houseboat people settled down in their new surroundings.

A young girl once applied for a position as a ward-maid at the nearby Hamadryad Hospital, one of the island's landmarks. She was a little shy as to her actual address and simply put Rose Cottage, The Docks, Cardiff. She was engaged on a month's trial and proved a very capable and punctual worker. It was not until she had been at the hospital for some time that the authorities discovered that Rose Cottage was one of the houseboats and came in some concern to the matron. She was adamant, however, that the girl must stay. 'She has proved herself', she said firmly, 'the houseboat may lack conveniences but she is as clean as a new pin'. And stay she did. The Hamadryad with its good old surgical smell was a fascinating place for us, although for the most part we were only on the outside looking in. We imagined the seamen to be suffering from all kinds of strange wounds or tropical diseases. Men groaned, swathed in bandages, suffering from scalds caused by the almost daily boiler explosions on the dirty tramp steamers sailing under sealed orders. Through the influence of twopenny books like the *Rover* and *Wizard*, we saw the captains as bearded toughs with bloodshot eyes all working for some tucked-away office in London which masqueraded under a false name. The crews of these ships were half-starved, bullied and often wounded as they were forced to work for the brutal officers because of some secret in their past life. All kinds of diseases, however, were treated at the hospital. I sang carols with St Stephen's Choir there. We used to robe ourselves in the staffroom and on one of these occasions as I was chatting to one of the nurses I decided to check up on these knifing stories. 'What', I asked her, 'were most of the patients in the hospital suffering from?'. She answered vaguely that they suffered from lots of different illnesses; but I persisted. 'Were many of them wounded or recovering from knife wounds?', I asked. She smiled and said that many were indeed wounded and had certainly suffered from some knife cuts,

but the wounds were not in the places we would imagine them to be. I remember telling my father when I got home and I can recall him laughing to this day.

The Hamadryad, now a red-brick hospital, was originally a ship, a naval frigate brought to Cardiff in 1866. The immediate cause was an outbreak of ship's fever in the early 1816s and the Corporation had begged the naval authorities for a ship they could use as a seamen's hospital. Many of the old folk of the docks can still remember the ship hospital for it was not replaced until the turn of the century. Like the famed *Temeraire* painted by Turner, she too faded up the river as she was towed away about to be broken up, but nobody painted a picture of her. Her contribution, however, to the suffering seamen of Cardiff will be remembered for all time.

In the less organised days of medicine the old ship hospital would treat the local people with twopenny bottles of medicine and pennyworth's of pills. When many doctors demanded that you cross their palms with three and sixpence before they passed the threshold, the ship's doctor must have fulfilled a very real need.

I was a small boy when a terrible disaster struck the locality. The Clarence Road Bridge was being painted by a family firm from Scotland. The ropes holding the cradles from which the bridge was being painted broke and the men were hurled into the liquid mud of the low tide below. A rescue operation was mounted and the men were rushed to the Hamadryad. Nurse John, later to become Matron, was just returning from town on a tram. As it rattled over the bridge she could see that something was up. The tram slowed down before it reached the end of the bridge so she jumped off and raced down Clarence Embankment hearing pieces of the story from bystanders. There wasn't time for her to change into nurses' uniform and still in her summer dress she flung herself into efforts to revive the men by extracting the black mud from their throats and nostrils. It was a hopeless task from the beginning, but the brothers and cousins of the men standing by agreed something had to be done. They worked for hours and she remembers her dress was soaked in perspiration and mud. It was one of the saddest moments in the history of the hospital.

It is hard to imagine the poverty of the 1920s today. I can remember boys hanging around better-off children hoping there would be something left from the mid-morning lunches. Even the edge of a crust was welcome. Children came to school in leaky boots with the uppers parting from the soles, and many without stockings. In fact the first time many of them wore stockings was when they played for the school football team. The stockings with the shirt and knicks, would be given out on Friday and collected on Monday. It was nothing to see children hobbling to school in ladies' shoes. Often these children were blue with cold, the wind whistling through their ragged trousers and their feet cut and festering. I remember Miss Brotherton, the headteacher of Clarence Road Infants School, who must have used miles of bandage and dressings patching up children. She was a wonderful person dedicated to teaching and she certainly made her school a place for children to remember. Children would beg in the evenings at the dock gates for leavings and many knew more dinner-times than dinners. At five to twelve some of the very poor children were called out to receive little green dinner-cards that entitled them to four-penn'orth of food from Leyshon's Restaurant in James Street. This was often soup, bread, pasty and a cake. I remember coming home from playing football one Saturday morning to find a neighbour in great distress. Saturday mid-day her husband had rolled in having spent or gambled every penny of his pay. All he had brought home was a cabbage, which he tossed to her saying 'Boil that for the children's dinner'. When she began to argue with him about having to try and live for a week on nothing, he had thrown her out into the street and then in a black fit of temper had started breaking up all the crockery in the kitchen dresser. My mother urged my father to go and do something about it and I well remember his

words. 'Let him have his fit out. He'll sleep it off presently and with luck will wake up with some sense in his head. Then I'll go and have a chat with him'. I have heard of other men who wouldn't go home after losing most of their wages at cards or on the horses. They would hang about hoping to find a pal from whom they could borrow. My father often had such friends calling in from time to time glad to have a cup of tea and something to eat, and a place to sit for a while. My mother, who controlled the purse strings, like most women of the day, would warn my father not to part with anything, but he invariably did. Early one Saturday evening he was taking my mother on their weekly visit to town when he met a man he had befriended not many hours before waiting outside the *Avondale* public house. He straightened up when he saw my father. 'I'm a disgrace, Jim', he said, 'I'll never learn', and he never did.

Police rarely interfered between man and wife. My father often related the story of a young constable new to the docks who entered a house to stop a man seemingly beating his wife to death. As he began to handle the husband, the woman he was trying to defend drove a hat-pin into him, and called him some choice names. As one older constable told my father, 'They're best

Pride in every line as the author's father (*right*), with friend, pose in a Bute Street photographer's studio for this bicycling study, *c*.1901

left alone Jim—they are the worst of enemies to-night—but they will be the best of married couples tomorrow'.

The general poverty of the 'twenties affected schoolboy sport. There was little help from the authority and schoolmasters tried everything. They collected coupons from porridge packets—one famous brand offered a free football for two hundred coupons. Jam-jar collecting was another project—I believe the going rate was four jars for a penny. Collecting cards were often distributed, usually consisting of the school stamp on a postcard and marked with lines accordingly. It was mostly halfpennies and pence with the occasional threepenny piece—but it all helped.

When the schoolboy baseball league was started in Cardiff in 1922 the Welsh Baseball Union offered their help to the extent of a 15/- grant to enable a school to purchase a bat and a ball. St Cuthbert's School in Pomeroy Street had entered the league and made the usual application for the grant. This was forthcoming but the following season the school did not apply to join the league. Mr Evan Llewellyn was the chairman of the league and he was from the Grange Council School. One dinner-time he accordingly called to see the headmistress regarding the position of the bat and ball. He noted with some concern that the bat and ball, still in good condition, were being used in the school yard. However, all ended well. The reason for not entering the league was that the football team shirts which also doubled for baseball were just hanging in shreds despite patching and darning. The school card collection had not yielded anything like enough money for a new set so very reluctantly they had to withdraw. Mr Llewellyn was a teacher of the old school. He believed in the maxim that a boy should be taught at one end and beaten on the other, what went on in between was education. One can picture the scene in those grim days, both teachers fingering the ragged shirts. Mr Llewellyn then looked out of the window at the boys and girls playing a game they obviously enjoyed and said, 'If it's only a question of a set of shirts, I'll see

what can be done'. A week later a parcel was brought from Grange by one of his senior pupils, with a set of shirts, newly removed from a secondhand shop in Grange; not new but in sound condition, and an old bat and tennis ball. A stickler for how equipment should be used, Mr Llewellyn suggested that the old bat would be best for use in the yard and that a tennis ball would be better as the hard surface would cut the stitches on the real baseball. After all, baseballs were half-a-crown each! So St Cuthbert's battled on as one of the pioneers of schoolboy baseball, and it is to the credit of these dockland teachers that without a field of any kind they were all in the league playing football and baseball.

St Cuthbert's, Clarence Road, and Eleanor Street, one Catholic, one 'Proddie', and one in between. Eleanor had a famous rallying call E-L-E-A-N-O-R . . . they would spell out as they carried the school goalposts from the school across to the Marl in Grangetown ending with the word 'Eleanor'! Besides organised games at school there were the games and pastimes of the street. Everything seemed to go in seasons. There weren't proper dates but suddenly at particular times the street would buzz with some new activity and everyone had to be in on the act. I suppose the appearance in the little shops of a halfpenny top and a penny whip would set that particular pastime under way and conkers naturally belonged to late September. But what about hoops, for nearly every family had at least one of a sort? There were wooden ones, solid bicycle wheels, and some steel ones with handles attached, the product of the shipyard. Children would run for hours with their hoops and racing somebody else around the block was a thrill worth savouring.

Cigarette cards have been described as the poor man's art gallery. They were a magical world to us kids and empty cigarette packets were eagerly pounced upon. Photos we all called them and I suppose they covered every subject under the sun. Film stars, sportsmen, especially cricketers, butterflies, flags, Kings and Queens, speed cars, famous ships and trains, racehorses and greyhounds, famous boxers, were some of the best-known runs. Some firms supplied albums and some children were diligent enough to fill them up carefully and look after them. But for most of us they represented the real currency of the streets especially when there wasn't too much of the minted kind around. We played all kinds of games with them, swapped them and one boy sold them fifty for a halfpenny—goodness knows where he obtained his supplies. In school there were photo bookies, strictly illegal of course, who ran books on the big races. They took their cut, ten cards in the hundred.

Alleys we played along the gutter or rolled them into the ring. In many other places I've heard them called glass marbles. Marbles to us were the clay variety with hard shiny surfaces. Street games rarely changed over the years. Talking to Mr Tom Letton of Clarence Embankment he recalled the games he played in the

streets of Rat Island at the turn of the century. He vividly remembers night rugby with the old gas lamps as 'floodlights' and a rolled up bundle of old books tied with string as the ball. Very different from some of the modern concepts of the game. Then there was a game of 'chukey'—a kind of chasing game 'Longey Last Lamp'—a competition to see who could touch the most lamp-posts in a given area of several streets. He attended Bute Town School in Mount Stuart Square and recalls there weren't any organised games at the school. When the school closed he moved to the old Clarence Road School. He vividly remembers one golden Friday afternoon when a ball was produced by the teacher and an organised game resulted. 'We talked about it for weeks', he told me, and the game became a monthly treat; providing behaviour and attendance was up to the required standard. Crowds of children would troop to the Marl on Saturday

'Huge crowds gathered as the walkers set out . . .' Here the Docks' Temperance Institute line up for the start of their second annual marathon race on Good Friday, 25 March 1910

17

Walking the greasy pole at the Cardiff Regatta

afternoons to watch Docks United in the winter and Grange Albion in the summer. Harry Buley and Freddie Fish both played for the Albion, Freddie once hitting nine fours as last man, a world record it was always said.

Tom remembers the excitement of the old walks organised by the workmen's club and held at holiday time. Huge crowds gathered as the walkers set out from some given point usually outside the club, or just by the canal's James Street Bridge. The *Merrie Harriers* and back was the usual destination and some it was said never came back, at least not for some time. Then there were the regattas held on the canal itself, races between such swimmers as Billy Kimber and Billy Smith, rowing races between coal-trimmers using their shovels for oars. The local children would watch goggle-eyed as a walk-the-plank contest was held

between a sweep and a miller but the event they all waited for was walking the greasy pole. This was always arranged pretty near the bank of the canal for a good reason. Hidden away were a quantity of small bags containing soot and sand and as the aspiring pole walkers started on their difficult task there were plenty of small boys ready to pelt the competitors.

Regattas were also held in front of the dock gates before tremendous crowds with races organised from the docks to Penarth. Tom can remember running amongst the crowd selling hat-guards at twopence each, these were strong attachments to keep straw hats from blowing away, for the docks even in the summer could be very windy.

Local boxers were treated as heroes although there wasn't television to publicise their fights.

A local favourite was Fred Dyer known as the 'singing boxer'. After winning his fights, Fred used to sing 'Thora', Tom told me. One night he was knocked out and his opponent stood over him and said 'Now you so-and-so what about singing Thora?'. Fred was a good-hearted fellow who rallied other boxers to stage a benefit fight for 'Peerless' Jim Driscoll before he sailed to America in 1909. Jim himself trained in the *North and South* public house in Louisa Street in a room which was christened the Blood Kitchen.

Most of these boxers would do anything for a good cause and of course Jim Driscoll's generosity is legendary. 'A featherweight inside the ring but a heavyweight outside', Tom said of him. 'All on account of the size of his heart'.

Many stories are told of Jim's open-handedness, but my personal memory concerns my father. Just before the first World War he had started up his own manufacture of oil-skin wet weather clothing for seamen. He invented a patent jacket which worked on the principal of self-inflation. To advertise it Jim, a well-known figure, was prepared to jump into the West Dock Basin when a ship was coming in, and the area would be fairly alive with people. He would shout for help, and then save himself by blowing up the jacket through the tube provided. Unfortunately at the

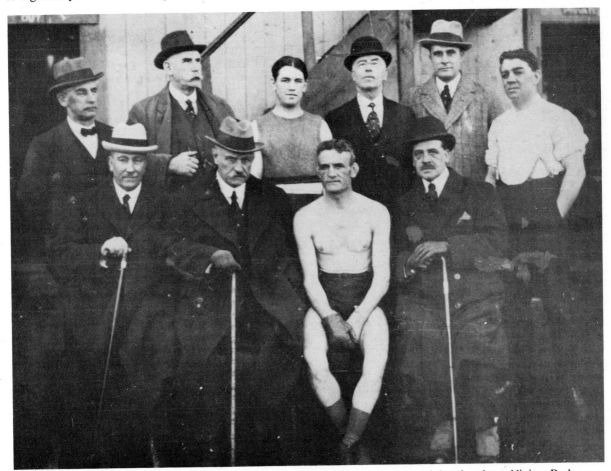

'Peerless' Jim Driscoll, looking far from fit, photographed during a training break at Ninian Park football ground shortly before his last fight. Cardiffians still talk about Jim's kindness and generosity

appointed time Jim was taken ill, but my father never forgot what he tried to do for a pal. Like many Rat Island folk my father was one of the huge crowd that saw Jim take his last journey in February 1925, when pneumonia dealt the knockout blow to a man who will be talked about as long as men wear prize gloves.

Rat Island abounded with characters. Joe Evans, a lock-keeper known as 'Joe the Beef' or just 'Joe Beef'. Andrew Bloater who had a strange-shaped face—one half of which resembled a pig. He sold the *South Wales Echo* and walked with a strange little hop. It was always said that poor Andrew had sold his head to the Infirmary for £1,000. As little kids we used to gaze after him trying to imagine such a vast amount of money. It was said that pregnant women would hide themselves when Andrew came down the street afraid that the sight of him would affect their babies.

Near Clarence Bridge a man used to stand gazing at the river and talking to people nobody else could see. He was called 'Cabbage-lips', did nobody any harm and existed in a dream world of his own imagination.

A great deal of Rat Island is still in existence. True the canal is gone—replaced by a green lane of grass—giving dockland children a place to play, and the timber-floats have disappeared. But Dumballs Road, the Hamadryad, the *Avondale* pub, the *New Sea Lock*, the V shaped Conservative Club are all still there.

As Tom Letton, who sold fish for nearly forty years around the island said, 'It's a warm friendly place to live and I wouldn't want to live anywhere else'.

The Railway Mission

by Elizabeth Dart

WHEN THE FIRST railway 'navvies' had been recruited from the former canal 'navigators', it was not long before earnest Victorian social workers discovered a mission to regulate the lives of those men of strong passions and powerful thirsts. After they had been successfully calmed and converted, and some persuaded to marry their camp followers whether they were really willing or not, then the kindly attention was diverted to railway families, while goodness and charity spread all along the iron roads as they reached out across the country and down the years.

White kid boots and a straw hat trimmed with daisies, a hymn book and a handkerchief and a penny for the collection, a small wooden chair to stand on while I piped the weighty words of the hymns; these are my earliest recollections of the Railway Mission. It happened every Sunday evening in the upstairs room of a shop in Ninian Park Road. Across the road loomed Victoria Baptist where I spent Sunday mornings and afternoons and many Tuesday evenings at the Band of Hope being put off liquor for life. Peering reprovingly round Wells Street corner was St Cadoc's C. of E., where I was christened. Mine was a tolerant family.

I was much older when I discovered that Ninian Park Road had once been called Eldon Street, named, no doubt, after the Lord Eldon who firmly believed in the retention of the feudal system because he thought people were happier that way. Unfortunately, the enthusiastic activities of a number of professional ladies brought a bad reputation to the name of Eldon Street, and in 1924 a petition by 166 ratepayers was sent to the City Council for the name to be changed. Now it was hallowed by hymns, patrolled by the Salvation Army; virtue and Bible verses had conquered vice.

What was there so special about railway workers that they should have had a brand of evangelism all to themselves? Why did religion go along with railway engines, except that the same kind of dedication seemed to be given to both? Gathered in that stuffy room on so many sleepy Sunday evenings in the peaceful days between one war and the thought of another, were the wives and children of engine drivers, firemen and the fitters who kept the wheels turning. They might be driving and firing and fitting in their oily overalls, but we would be there in our very best, listening to talks on 'When you reach the points will you switch to the Up Line or the Down Line?', or descriptions of those many mansions that are waiting for us, all complete with large railway station type entrance halls with massive marble pillars.

This small upper room had the railway line running along behind it, so that at regular intervals a passing train would completely cancel our prayers—'Give us a signal, Lord', and 'God grant us peace'.

As a relief from all these railway images there was a large coloured print on the wall for the children's benefit, and I stared at it for so many sleepy, sooty, engine-shed smelling Sunday evening hours that it is engraved on my mind to this day. You know it, of course; it shows the Friend of little children, handsome and tanned, seated with young people of all nations in clean, tidy national costumes gathered around. A coloured boy, rather bare, has the place of honour on His lap, but in the curve of His arm is an old-fashioned dainty English miss, all fair curls, pink sash and frills. I never doubted that her father worked on the railway.

Suddenly there would be a shattering crash of buffers from outside; everyone would jerk to attention and the speaker was off again—'The Lord will be your Guard'. God was in His smoky Heaven, shunting the world along, and all was safe and secure in the shadow of the Great Western Railway.

There was a monthly magazine, called *The Railway Signal*, brought by the Mission's most devoted worker, an upright lady with a stern, dedicated face, that always made me think of the Lady with the Oil Lamp. Her firm knock on the door would make us all rush round stuffing the Sunday newspapers under the cushions, to appear panting and impatient for the latest pale blue inspiring issue of *The Railway Signal*.

She had such a single track mind about helping the railway workers on their journey through life that she must have convinced them that every night train to Paddington might be their last. During meal breaks she had permission to go into the 'cabin' and lead drivers, firemen and fitters in prayer. On one sad occasion when she had them all down on their knees with eyes closed while she prayed for guidance, their longing for a billy-can full of strong tea proved too much, and one by one they silently crawled out on all fours. When she finished her prayers and opened her eyes she was alone—and things were never the same again. Everyone was sorry, my father said, but nothing was as rigid as a railway timetable in those days, and a man had to stoke himself up as well as the engine.

Railways and respectability seem to have gone together since the very beginning; one of the first railway engineers in South Wales was Joseph Benjamin Hemingway, a cousin of my great-great grandfather, and like him a native of Yorkshire. He prospered, and lived at Quarry Hill House, Mount Pleasant, St Mellons, which has become an Old People's Home. Now he lies peacefully outside the church door at St Mellons, under an imposing monument which bears the proud inscription 'Railway Contractor'.

My father must have felt the same sort of pride when as a special treat he sometimes led me over the bridge from the street to the engine sheds. There were no trumpets sounding on the other side, only train whistles and the crash of bumpers as I was led to admire his favourite engines while he lovingly wiped them over with a soft piece of oily waste. He could hardly wait to present his grandson, aged three at the time, with an elaborate set of model engines and a complicated track, and who am I to complain of several tense years spent rescuing expensive rolling stock from tiny battering fists?

I am glad my father never saw the tourists lost in admiration near the forgotten rusting railway lines behind Barry station, where now stand the last of those familiar cherished engines, no longer glossy, no longer proudly steaming, but neglected, dull, dejected, awaiting execution and annihilation.

I never heard of anyone feeling religious about diesels, did you?

We Taught the Yanks the Ancient Sport of Baseball

by Bob Evans

ROUNDERS, AS BASEBALL was known in its early years, has probably been played on every village green and common since Tudor times. It was one of the games banned in the Middle Ages because it interfered with the sport of archery, so vital to Britain's defences at that time. In the 18th century the name of baseball was not new in this country. In the letters of Mary Lepell, Lady Harvey, there occurs a passage under the date 8 November 1748 satirising Frederic, Prince of Wales, and his moronic habits . . . 'The Prince's family is an example of cheerful and innocent amusements . . . they divert themselves to baseball; a play all who are, or have been, schoolboys, are well acquainted with'.

It is claimed that John Chadwick, an Exeter journalist and member of the Gloucester Rounders' Association, emigrated to America in 1772 and introduced the game there, only for it to return a century later in a glamourised 'Yankee' form. In 1774 a pocket book was published in England, which later became very popular in America. It was an illustrated alphabet with crude woodcuts of 26 children's sports, one for each letter of the alphabet. 'B' represented baseball and the illustration showed that the batter hit the ball and ran from base to base. Here again is evidence that even the *name* baseball was introduced to America!

In *Northanger Abbey* written by Jane Austen about 1798 we read about her heroine as follows: 'it was not very wonderful that Catherine, who had by nature nothing heroic about her, should prefer cricket, baseball, riding on horseback and running around the country at the age of fourteen to books'.

There is little evidence of any real organisation about the sport in this country in those far-off days but it was certainly popular in Merseyside, Gloucester, Scotland and South Wales. Over 150 clubs were playing in 1868 and their leagues were known as rounders.

Hilda Royle, now Mrs Pill, was one of the pioneers of baseball in Cardiff. She is seen in action for Ladies' Baptist Institute

23

Grange Baptists and Penarth Ladies before a league match in 1926

In 1892 Liverpool Rounders' Association at their annual meeting took the revolutionary step of changing officially the name of rounders to baseball. This was adopted as being more appropriate to the skilful style of play being developed. In the same year South Wales changed the name of the Rounders' League to Baseball League and as a result American sides toured England in the hope of converting the population to their game, without however reaching Wales. In 1888 two touring teams of American professionals—the Chicago National League and the All Americans—had arrived in England and played games at the Oval and in other areas. This left its mark on the North of England and the Midlands. Even today Derby County's football ground is known as the Baseball Ground. The English sides, however, who had played both styles, regardless of rules and regulations, had sorted themselves out and British baseball took on a definite pattern. Wales too was little troubled by the propaganda visits and although an American League was formed in Cardiff just

before the Second World War it had hardly any effect on the Welsh game.

To revert back for a moment, the change from rounders to baseball did not take place in South Wales until June 1892 when the parent body, the South Wales Association, was formed. It was significant that whereas England taught Wales rounders and were the masters, their playing style even at the first international match in 1908 still retained rounders features, notably one handed batting, but the Welsh game had completely changed. As the game spread the Welsh Baseball Association was formed in 1912 which directly controlled all games and clubs in the Monmouthshire Association and the Cardiff and District League. In 1921 the existing Welsh Baseball Union was formed creating a Welsh League of the leading clubs. Also into being came the Cardiff and District (Wednesday) League and a Sunday Schools' League. Each league became a separate entity controlling its own affairs but with direct representation to the Council of the Welsh Baseball Union.

Wales and England had little in common from 1890 until 1907 when the idea of an international match was made a reality in the next season. However, it was not the first time that representative teams had played. In 1880 East London beat Canning Town by 22 runs, and in the same year Liverpool defeated Gloucester by 72 runs. In 1893 there is a record of Liverpool also beating Glasgow. The teams then playing in South Wales incuded St Woolos of Newport, Pillgwently, Canton YMCA, Castle Gardeners, the Electricity Club, Grangetown and Newport. Trophies played for were the Cardiff Athletic Shield and the South Wales Challenge Shield, won by Cardiff in 1890 and Newport in the following year. Interest was now mounting and a Rounders' League was formed composed of teams called Cardiff, Canton, Penarth, Upper and Lower Grange, with extra sides coming in later from Newport, Abertridwr and Gloucestershire. Prior to this, about 1873, large crowds gathered on the now historic Marl, Grangetown. In between sessions of pitch and toss, baseball was played and a round shaft of wood, just over a yard long, nicknamed a 'Timmy' was used as a bat. The ball was wound with elastic and would race over the hard clay surface for some quarter of a mile, often unwinding itself as it bounced along.

In 1922 it was the turn of the schoolboys and the Cardiff Schools' Association was formed, followed a year later by the Newport Schools' League. This caught on and was repeated in Caerphilly, Bridgend, Treorchy, Aberdare, Barry and Pontypridd.

The ladies of Cardiff took a hand in 1923 and set up a friendly team in the Grangetown area of the city and formed the Cardiff and District Ladies' League. Competing in those days were Grange Wesleyans, Docks Ladies, Cornwall Road Baptists, Grange Albion, Grange Baptists, Rose of Cardiff, Grange Ladies and Grange Mills.

The game carried on successfully in the 'twenties and 'thirties and on the resumption after the war the Welsh Baseball Union took control of the whole of baseball. The old Cardiff and District League became part of the Welsh National League with the Union the top body—which it still is today.

Grange Albion dominated the post-war scene until Penylan took over in the 'fifties. It was then that a new bowler of rare talent emerged. His name was John Clements and at 16 years of age he was the fastest the game had ever seen. He attracted the attention of the Welsh selectors and soon won himself a trial. He was such a success that he bowled out the Probables and the Possibles with such speed that Wales knew at last they had

Charlie Williams (Penylan) batting and A. Smith (Grange Albion) backstop at the opening of the Welsh Baseball Union cup final at St Saviour's ground, Pengam, Cardiff in 1933
Photograph courtesy Western Mail & Echo Ltd

a bowler who could be pitted against England and stem the rising tide of English supremacy.

The author will never forget the game at Stanley Greyhound Track, Liverpool, in 1951. Clements had a wonderful debut bowling unchanged in

Doug Lloyd, Grange Albion's bowler, in action in 1949
Photograph courtesy Western Mail & Echo Ltd

both innings. England crumbled and in 45 minutes they were out for 20 and 14. Wales romped home by an innings. In the following year at Sophia Gardens, Cardiff, the crowds flocked to see Clements in action against England once again. Could he repeat his performance? He soon gave the answer as Wales registered another innings victory and England were tumbled out for 20 and 20.

His impact on the game was terrific and the team that signed Clements scooped the trophies. The accent was now on speed but, unfortunately, it became speed at a price and bowlers unable to match the genius of Clements resorted to throwing. Controversy raged week after week as doubtful bowlers were called for no-balling, but Clements went on. Then on the scene came controversial stylist Paddy Hennessey who could match Clements for speed and skill. He won his first cap at Edinburgh Park, Liverpool, in 1957, but after taking 7 for 33 he was repeatedly no-balled and was taken out of the bowling box. Wales coasted home with Clements finishing off the remaining England batsmen.

So to the following year and Maindy Stadium, Cardiff. The Welsh attack consisted of Clements and Hennessey and the crowds flocked to see this Golden Jubilee game. They were not disappointed. The chief guest was Lance Ramsey, the only English survivor from the 1908 game to see his son Eric play. On his own ground Hennessey was not no-balled and England were humiliated once again as the two Welsh bowlers ripped England apart for 27 and 17. Although Clements went on to win ten international caps it was the last international appearance for Hennessey. Despite his whirlwind action he had contributed much to the game and crowds gathered every Saturday to see these two personalities in club matches.

As already stated, it was in 1908 when the international series commenced between Wales and England with the first game being played at the Old Harlequins ground, Cardiff. Wales emerged the winners and it is interesting to note

Successful Splott U.S. team in 1952
Photograph courtesy Western Mail & Echo Ltd

that the rules for the first time were changed to accommodate the visitors.

There were two umpires, one behind the bowling box and one level with the batting crease, but this was not always a success. They often disagreed and the game would be thrown into confusion. Since then only one umpire has been in charge of a game. Both countries have met once a year on a home and away basis, with only the two world wars intervening.

Wales have generally held the upper hand but England had their best run when they won five games in succession between 1935 and 1939 with two of the matches being played on the sacred turf of Cardiff Arms Park. The narrowest victory in the series was in 1932 and it is well worth recording the last moments of that epic game.

England required only seven runs for victory when Joe Deegan went to the pegs, but he had to strike to get his three team mates home, who were all holding bases. The Welsh crowd was hushed as Harry Buley, the Welsh pitcher, bowled. Deegan took a big swipe missed the ball and it was in the diamond before the player on number three could move.

It was a sensational game throughout for in the first innings England batsman R. McQueen was given out by an unsighted umpire despite strong appeals from the England team. The ball had in fact been thrown to the fielder by a spectator, but the umpire stood by his first decision and McQueen was out.

There have been many notable internationals for Wales. Lew Lewis was the first captain of his country, Buzzer Heaven, the backstop who once put out four men with one ball, and Harry Davies who scored the first pair of ducks in the series, a feat equalled by many since.

There was Dai Davies who became the first player to hit 100 runs in the series, bowler Arthur Mitchell, Carl Grey still considered by many as the fastest player of all time. Grange Albion's Fred Hayes, another fine backstop Charlie Williams, Percy Smith, Danny Dowd, Tommy Denning, and superb fielders Harry Gardiner, W. 'Pablo' Manley from Newport and Reg St Clare, Bobby Roper, Penylan's body line bowler, and Ted Peterson another fine Penylan sportsman. Others include Fred Fish and Dai Charles, Arthur Noyes, Don O'Leary, Doug Lloyd, all of Grange Albion. Then in the last 20 years, there have been Clements, Hennessey, hard hitting Jackie Thompson, Terry Slocombe,

Graham Pymble and Ray Knight, just to name a few.

According to American records, the father of baseball was rounders, carried to the North American continent by English colonists. The children of these pioneers grew to manhood playing the game and rounders changed from a child's frolic into a keen competition, in which skill had to be met with skill. In New England and the Maritime Provinces of Canada it was called variously 'Rounders', 'Round Ball' and 'Town Ball', the latter name surviving until 1850. In Northern New York State the game took on the names of 'One Old Cat', 'Two Old Cat' etc, this probably some reference to 'Dog and Cat', a variety of rounders played in England some years previously.

Rules varied with the locality, and discipline was not a primary consideration. The game was

Fairoak baseball side in 1955. They won the Welsh Baseball Union Cup and *Empire News* Cup
Photograph courtesy Western Mail & Echo Ltd

Arthur Noyes (Grange Albion) turns away when bowled by John Clements. Behind is Bryn Richards the Fairoak backstop. Action from a 1956 league match
Photograph courtesy Western Mail & Echo Ltd

generally accompanied with the hilarity and horse-play of childhood days. It was not necessary to touch an advancing baserunner with the ball to retire him and part of the fun and excitement was to watch fielders throw the ball at the runner to put him out, often with very serious results.

In 1845 the first 'real' club was organised. It printed a rule book, and as time went on, other clubs conformed to these rules, which until the late 'nineties, changed with greater frequency. There is no record of the name of 'baseball' being first adopted and this was probably a compromise of the many names extant. Up to 1863 a base-runner could run on a foul ball and prior to 1864 a batsman was out if a fielder caught his batted ball on the first bounce.

Eight years later the modern ball was brought in, which is practically the same size and weight as a cricket ball. Catchers complained that these broke their noses more often than the original balls, and three years later the mask was invented. During the same year gloves also appeared. These were derisively called 'pillows' by hard-boiled veterans, who displayed with pride their gnarled and bent fingers. Later an Irish catcher, inspired by cricket, invented shin guards.

Up to 1876 it remained doubtful if baseball would ever become organised, but the year saw the birth of the National League, which for some time ruled the game with an iron hand in America and Canada.

The sport, claim the Americans, was not entirely new in England and had been played consistently in the villages around Chipping Norton, Oxford-shire since 1912. It is claimed that a scoutmaster of that town, Fred Lewis, found an American rule book and although he had never seen the game played, found no difficulty in introducing it to the boys.

Entirely self-taught it is understood that Chipping Norton and district had several times beaten the best talent London could muster from resident Canadians and Americans. The lore of the district

Fred Hayes of Grange Albion at the pegs in 1956
Photograph courtesy Western Mail & Echo Ltd

Ken Hollyman, captain of Penylan, receives the *Empire News* Cup from Maureen Staffer, then of TWW. The game was played at Maindy Stadium in 1960
Photograph courtesy Western Mail & Echo Ltd

has it that Doubleday of 'One Old Cat' fame was not born in New York State at all, but in Woodstock, Oxfordshire, and that his version of the game was a traditional sport of the Cotswolds. It is also recorded in Oxfordshire that nearly 200 years ago some village people were put in the stocks for 'Plaeynge at Towne Balle on the Sabbath'.

But what of the future of 'our' game? There is little chance of it spreading outside its present narrow limits for it is still confined to Cardiff, Newport and Liverpool. In its present form it requires a piece of ground really larger than a football pitch. Many towns in the valleys have been eager to take up the sport, but space has been the problem. If some far-seeing legislator could reduce the game to the size of an average soccer or rugby pitch then baseball would have the opportunity of spreading.

One suggestion is that there should be no scoring strokes over the backstop's head and scoring strokes would be between one and three base, but top officials have not taken kindly to this suggestion.

Grange Albion team in 1958

Photograph courtesy Western Mail & Echo Ltd

When Legal History Was Made in Cardiff

The story of a brilliant but tragic judge
by Elizabeth Dart

ON THURSDAY 12 February **1884**, an excited crowd was waiting for the start of the Glamorgan Winter Assizes in Cardiff, where a confrontation was about to take a place between a judge with a remarkable reputation, and a well known local character who was just as inflexible in his own very individual way. Hanging and quartering and eye gouging had gone out of fashion, but everyone felt that something dramatic was about to happen

The judge was Sir James Fitzjames Stephen, who had been successively Recorder of Newark upon Trent; Legal Member of the Council of the Governor General of India; Professor of Common Law at the Inns of Court; Judge of the High Court of Justice since 1879, and author of many works on the law, including *A General Review of Criminal Law* (1863); *Digest of Criminal Law* (1877); and *Digest of the Laws of Evidence* (1876).

And the trial was that of Dr William Price of Llantrisant, who was 84 years of age and had been accused of attempting to burn the body of his infant son instead of burying it. A second indictment charged him with attempting to burn the body with intent to prevent the holding of an inquest upon it.

Dr Price was respected for his eccentricity; my grandmother was proud to say that he was once pointed out to her in Cardiff Market. It was impossible to mistake him, they said, because he dressed in a highly individual manner, favouring a green coat and trousers with a red waistcoat, and a cap made from a fox skin with the tail all complete hanging down at the back.

The judge, who was said to have conducted the case magnificently, seemed very taken with the stalwart old man. Addressing the jury, he remarked that the question was whether the burning of a dead body was to be treated as a crime. For his own part he entertained the strongest opinion that it was not the duty of the judges of the land to invent new crimes. A practice had been introduced which broke no law he **knew** of, a practice which might be so followed—he only said 'might be'—as to shock no man's feelings and which it was not even challenged did any great mischief whatsoever. That we were all mortal, and that our bodies must sooner or later be returned to the elements of which they are composed was, no doubt, a fact, and the process by which this was done must always be horrible to think of. He did not see himself, if the thing was done decently, that burning a body was more horrible than burying it . . . His opinion was, that the mere burning of a body was not an offence; that if, on the other hand, it was burnt in such a manner as to give ordinary persons reasonable ground of offence, then it was a misdemeanour. When he said 'ordinary persons' he used the words for this reason.

There were some people in the world who took offence at their neighbours doing anything which they did not do themselves, or which was not according to their own habits and practices, and there were many people extremely indignant as soon as they heard that anyone had political or religious opinions with which they did not agree, or were addicted to habits and ways of life which were considered absurd or wrong.

That was a habit not to be commended, and which the law of this country did not protect. Therefore, the mere fact that this person or that

31

might think the burning of a body wrong, or might have some religious scruples against this practice, was not what he referred to when he used the term 'giving offence to ordinary people's feelings'. He meant, first, 'offence to the senses', secondly he alluded to the feeling of respect and awe with which one looked upon a dead body. Those feelings were not to be wantonly interfered with, and if anyone wanted to burn a body they might do so, but they must take care to do so in the fullest sense of the words 'decently and in order', and in such a manner as not to offend neighbours. That, he thought, was the law, and he thought it was commonsense. Whether commonsense or not, in his judgement it was the law, and the gentlemen of the jury were bound for the purposes of that trial, as also were the learned counsel, to submit to his ruling upon the matter of law.

The jury retired, and after about three hours the foreman observed that there was no prospect of their agreeing on the matter. His Lordship dismissed them and announced his intention of holding a new trial the following morning.

Another jury after lunch was empanelled to hear evidence on the second indictment; that the defendant had disposed of the body of the child without certificate and without giving the coroner an opportunity of holding an enquiry or post mortem examination.

Dr Price gave a spirited address . . . 'The people followed the police and took me as if I had been a felon or a murderer, and took me from doing what has been practically done before, what I should have done by persons connected with me, and with myself, because I consider it a better mode of dealing with all persons than poisoning the earth, poisoning the water, and poisoning the atmosphere . . .'

The jury, after some confusion, found Dr Price 'Not Guilty', and the first charge was then withdrawn.

The judge finally addressed the jury . . .

I may say formally to you, but really to the defendant Price through you, that people may

Sir James Fitzjames Stephen, KCSI

hold the view that the practice of burning is better than the practice of burial; but we must remember what everybody who lives in the world would do well always to bear in mind, viz., that people ought to regard each other's feelings, and there is no subject in the world probably upon which mankind feels more strongly or naturally than upon the treatment of dead bodies. Feeling—I don't say it is altogether reasonable—I think it is not—but feeling is shocked at the burning of a body, although it may be an act of tenderness to prevent a more horrible process than that of burning . . . Therefore, if people determine to do this unusual act which is likely to be misunderstood and give offence to a great number of people who ought not to have offence given them, it is not only a legal, but, so far as I have a right to talk about it, a moral duty to use every possible means to prevent annoyance to the neighbours and to prevent their attention from being attracted to what was going on. With regard to Mr Price, he is acquitted. I am sure he must feel that he has been fairly treated on this occasion, and I hope that he will take what has been said in good part. He obviously enjoys much greater vigour, and has enjoyed much greater vigour, than falls to the lot of most of us. He has lived a great many years, and looks as if he will live many more. Although he expressed his intention of burning himself if he could not find anybody else to do it, I'm sure it is not his wish to give offence to his neighbours, and I trust that they, on the other hand, will tolerate an old man's eccentricities and peculiar views.

The Cremation Society of England was formed on 13 January 1874, and this was the test case they needed. Due to the social revolution pioneered by Dr Price and the sympathy of the judge, the first cremation was organised in 1885, at St John's, Woking. Cardiff's Thornhill Crematorium was opened on 30 November, 1953; twenty years later, in the year ending 31 March 1973, 2,973 cremations were carried out there with dignity and compassion, offending no one, as Mr Justice Stephen had so earnestly desired.

In 1885 Judge Stephen suffered a mental breakdown, but he was again in Cardiff in 1887, presiding over the trial known as Regina v. Ensor. This really concerned someone who is known by sight to everyone who has lifted his eyes when crossing the Hayes and observed the statue which stands there—John Batchelor, Mayor of Cardiff in 1854, Friend of Freedom. Born in Newport in 1820, he had settled in Cardiff and was a Radical Liberal, that is, a member of the Reforming party. His obituary in the *Western Mail* says: 'In all municipal and Parliamentary contests he was in the forefront of the battle', but he had made political enemies, which no doubt helped to account for the failure of his once prosperous ship-building business, and his financial difficulties. In 1872 he had to write to his 15-year-old son at boarding school and tell him that his future was uncertain.

'I feel dreadfully bad about poor papa's failure', confided the young Cyril to his diary. 'We are quite ruined'. But John Batchelor had not lost his friends; he kept his head high and managed to send his sons back to school. Cyril went on to a most successful career as one of the early railway engineers. His father died in 1883, and fellow Liberals decided to erect a statue in his honour. Their political opponents objected strongly to the site chosen on the Hayes, being expensive land recently acquired, and the statue itself when erected had to be given police protection. On 11 February 1887, Mr William Thorne was charged with defacing the statue by throwing paint and tar at it, and also with damaging a certain memorial to the dead. He was fined £15, to be paid to the Hamadryad Hospital ship.

But, more seriously, on 24 July 1886, the *Western Mail* printed the following mock epitaph for the statue, which had been sent to them by a local solicitor named Thomas Henry Ensor, who was quick to deny having written it two days later when he heard that Mr Batchelor's sons were said

John Batchelor (1820-83)
Photograph courtesy Cardiff Central Library

33

to have threatened him with assault.

'Our esteemed correspondent "Censor" sends us the following suggested epitaph for the Batchelor Statue:—

IN HONOUR
OF
JOHN BATCHELOR
A NATIVE OF NEWPORT
Who in early life left his country for his country's good;
Who, on his return, devoted his life and energies to setting
CLASS AGAINST CLASS
A Traitor to the Crown, a Reviler of the Aristocracy, A Hater of the Clergy,
A Panderer to the Multitude,
Who, as first Chairman of the Cardiff School Board, squandered funds to which he did not contribute:
Who is sincerely Mourned by Unpaid Creditors to the amount of
FIFTY THOUSAND POUNDS:
Who at the close of a wasted and mis-spent life Died a Demagogue and a Pauper,
THIS MONUMENT,
To the Eternal Disgrace of Cardiff,
Is Erected
BY SYMPATHETIC RADICALS:

'OWE NO MAN ANYTHING'

On 27 July, Mr Lascelles Carr, the editor of the *Western Mail*, was waylaid on his way to his office from the General Station by Cyril and his brother Llewellyn who were armed with a riding whip and a malacca cane. They were restrained before doing much damage to Mr Carr, and subsequently appeared in court. They were fined a nominal shilling without costs, and the magistrates condemned the mock inscription in no uncertain terms.

The words 'left his country for his country's good' were a quotation from the prologue of an old play about convicts transported to Australia, and were an oblique reference to John Batchelor's

The statue of John Batchelor 'The Friend of Freedom' on Hayes Island
Photograph by Haydn Baynham

34

brief connection with the Chartists in Newport, when he was 19-years-old. Mr Ensor had said this many years previously: in a letter to *The Reformer and South Wales Times*, dated 13 December 1861, he remarked, 'I was not such a fool as to "leave my country for my country's good" and with a view to escape the perilous consequences which might otherwise have resulted from my youthful indiscretions'. Protestations were made by Benjamin Matthews on behalf of John Batchelor, and a disclaimer was published four days later.

A test case such as this on the law of libel had been needed for some time, and it aroused great interest, not only in the town but in the whole country. Mr Justice Stephen held that a libel of the dead is not punishable, unless an intent to injure the living is proved.

'It is as safe to call one who died last year', he said, 'a liar and a murderer as it is to apply these epithets to Julius Caesar or Oliver Cromwell, but if by calling A (deceased) a murderer your intention is to imply that B (still living) is the son or brother of a murderer, you will be liable to punishment'.

Mr Bowen Rowlands, Q.C., for the defence, was able to quote from a book which the judge had previously written on criminal law:

Libel on dead men is not indictable unless it be proved that there is a criminal intent to harm the heirs, or unless it tends to cause a breach of the peace.

Ordering an acquittal the judge declared:

There must be a vilifying of the deceased with a view to injure his posterity. The dead have no rights and can suffer no wrongs. The living alone can be the subject of legal protection, and the law of libel is intended to protect them . . . It is sometimes said that, as a man must be held to intend the natural consequences of his acts, and as the natural consequence of the censure of a dead man is to exasperate his living friends and relations and so to cause breaches of the peace, attacks on the dead must be punishable as libels, because they tend to a breach of the peace whether they are or are not intended as an indirect way of reflecting on the living . . . but the intent to injure the family is a fact requiring proof and necessary to be found by the jury, and not an inference . . . from the terms of the writing reflecting on the dead man I am reluctant in the highest degree to extend the criminal law. To speak broadly, to libel the dead is not an offence known to our law.

The verdict did not pass without criticism. The *South Wales Daily News* of 12 February 1887, reprinted a comment which had appeared in *The Times* on the previous day:

. . . Cardiff seems to be a town in which party politics run high. Mr Batchelor's statue testifies to the existence of a strong Radical feeling among the inhabitants. The treatment it has received, apart from Mr Ensor's inscription for it, is equally clear—proof of an anti-Radical feeling at least equally strong. The offending stone has been daubed and painted and dishonoured in every possible way as a protest against the politics of its original, and a petition has been presented to the Town Council for its removal from public ground. It is important, says Mr Justice Stephen, in the interest of historical truth, that there should be free criticism of the dead. But what will the historian of the future be able to tell the world about Mr Batchelor? He will find proof on the one hand that he was a respected citizen of Cardiff, whose virtues while he was alive won the hearts even of his unpaid creditors, and who was honoured after his death with a public statue in memory of his good deeds, and as a perpetual injunction to others to follow in his footsteps. He will discover, on further research, very perplexing evidence to the contrary. In the *Western Mail* of 24 July 1886, he will read what 'Censor' had to say about his late fellow-townsman, and he will there see that the qualities which recommended Mr Batchelor to one class were viewed by another class in a wholly different light, and that they admit of being described in wholly different terms. If he gets no further than this somewhat lame conclusion, we fear that posterity will be left in ignorance of Mr Batchelor's actual merits or demerits, but we are not sure that they were so important an item in the history of the present age that the absence of authentic information about them will be very keenly felt, or that Mr Ensor's inscription was composed with a sole view of making up for the deficiency of other records. It may be safe to write libels about the dead, but it is not work which a man of delicate feeling would care to undertake, except as a public duty, and the inscription on Mr Batchelor's statue can hardly have been so motived.

And following is an extract from the *Cardiff Times and South Wales Weekly News* of Saturday, 19 February 1887:

Last week the Batchelor Libel Prosecution collapsed. The case did not break down because the evidence was inconclusive, but because Mr Justice Stephen interpreted the law in favour of the defendants, Carr and Ensor. According to the learned judge, the dead have no rights, and can suffer no wrong. This is a novel ruling, and is as startling as it is unsatisfactory. We wonder what the learned judge would think if someone proclaimed that his father was a liar and a thief. Such an allegation would be as devoid of truth as was every one of the shameful accusations hurled at the memory of John Batchelor. And Mr Justice Stephen, as a sound and consistent lawyer, would still cling to the conviction that the dead have no rights, and that it is not the duty of the living to preserve from desecration the tombs of those who have passed out of the world. There are several experienced judges who differ from Mr Justice Stephen, and should it be deemed advisable to obtain the ruling of the Court of Appeal it might be found that the law is not as Mr Justice Stephen understands it. While it is desirable that the utmost liberty should be accorded the historian, it is, nevertheless, a crying shame that any unscrupulous libeller

should have leave and licence to spread broadcast cruel falsehoods about a man who had lived a blameless life. If lawyers wish the public to respect the law, they should take care that the law accords more strictly with a sense of justice than has been revealed by the Batchelor prosecution.

To this 'historian of the future' the judge's words read like a poem. Indeed Judge Stephen did write poetry, so did John Batchelor, and so did the judge's second son, though his are the stuff of nightmares.

In a book by Michael Harrison, published in 1972, entitled *Clarence: the Life of H.R.H. the Duke of Clarence and Avondale* (1864-1892), the author declares that he is certain of the identity of that much-discussed murderer, 'Jack the Ripper'. (An even more convincing book came out in 1976, involving the painter Walter Sickert).

But Mr Harrison, in a very well reasoned summary of all the evidence, concludes that the 'Ripper' was James Kenneth Stephen, a handsome, well-built, brilliantly clever young man, who had been friend and tutor to the Duke of Clarence while he was at Cambridge. He received a blow on the head in an accident in 1886, which had unfortunate effects, but he also came from a family which had a history through several generations of strange 'mental breakdowns', usually referred to as 'severe illness caused by overwork'.

James Kenneth Stephen (said always to carry a sword stick) was the second son of a father who was well known in Cardiff—none other than Sir James Fitzjames Stephen—and he lived with his parents in Kensington. In the summer of 1888 his father appointed him Clerk of Assize for the South Wales Circuit, but he had various periods of illness which meant that he left all the actual work to his Deputy, and he resigned two years later.

His father, Sir James, according to Mr Harrison, having already had a mental breakdown, was also suffering from the strain caused by his son's strange 'lapses'. This seems to have become apparent during the trial in 1889 of Mrs Maybrick, who was accused of poisoning her husband with arsenic. She was found 'Guilty', but the sentence was afterwards commuted to life imprisonment, since many people believed her to be innocent, including the crowds at Liverpool, who treated the judge to such loud criticism that he had to be given a police escort.

Enough arsenic was found in Mrs Maybrick's house to poison fifty people, including a strong solution of milk and arsenic found in a tumbler in a hat box. Arsenic was also found when tests were done on a jug in which some lunch for her husband had been taken to his office. The attractive Mrs Maybrick explained that she used arsenic soaked from fly papers to beautify her skin. There was another man, of course.

Mr Justice Stephen, in his address to the jury, said:

You have to take off a good deal of discount from the testimony of skilled witnesses on the ground of their becoming, probably insensibly to themselves, advocates rather than witnesses . . . The subject and the evidence in this case is but one of the many instances which have satisfied me, if I had not already been satisfied of it before, that medicine and everything connected with medicine is so much a matter of fact, and experience of facts which do not readily present themselves for inspection, that you never can arrive at medical conclusions with anything like the same degree of certainty in your conclusions as you are entitled to expect in science which deals with mathematical demonstration or legal argument. I would not for the world say anything disrespectful of a science to which we all owe so very much, but it is a science based upon more or less conjecture, and good sense and good fortune in making guesses.

The columns of the old Town Hall in St Mary Street are just visible on the left of this *c*.1888 photograph.
It was in this building that legal precedents were set over ninety years ago
Photograph courtesy Cardiff Central Library

During this case it was obvious that the judge, to say the least, was finding it difficult to maintain his concentration. As his brother Leslie (afterwards Sir Leslie Stephen) wrote in the *Dictionary of National Biography*: 'A disease which had been slowly developing began to affect his mental powers. Upon hearing that public notice had been taken of supposed failure, he consulted his physician, and by his advice at once resigned in April, 1891'. He was made a baronet in recognition of his services, and he died at Ipswich in 1894.

His son James Kenneth died in a lunatic asylum in Northampton of 'Mania, 2½ months. Persistent refusal of food 20 days. Exhaustion', on 3 February 1892, which was three weeks after the death of his former friend and pupil, the Duke of Clarence.

On the death of Lord Russell of Killowen in 1900 (he had been Mrs Maybrick's defence counsel) the newspapers renewed their interest in the trial. In its issue of 13 August 1900, the *Liverpool Daily Post* printed the following:

In fancy one still hears the distant fanfare of the trumpets as the judges with quaint pageantry passed down the hall, and still with the mind's eye sees the stately crimson-clad figure of the great mad judge as he sat down to try his last case. A tragedy, indeed, was played upon the bench no less than in the dock.

Few who looked upon the strong, square head can have suspected that the light of reason was burning very low within; yet as the days of the trial dragged by—days that must have been as terrible to the judge as the prisoner—men began to nod at him, to wonder, and to whisper. Nothing more painful was ever seen in court than the proud old man's desperate struggle to control his failing faculties. But the struggle was unavailing. It was clear that the growing volume of facts was unassorted, undigested in his mind; that his judgement swayed backward and forward in the conflict of testimony; that his memory failed to grip the most salient features of the case for many

minutes altogether. It was shocking to think that a human life depended upon the direction of this wreck of what was once a great judge.

In fact, it was two years later that Judge Stephen saw a specialist, and as a result retired from the Bench. He was only sixty-two, but his judgements had continued to cause strong criticism, and he had twice been taken ill while on circuit.

The editor of the *Liverpool Daily Post* does not appear to have been prosecuted for what he had printed. This may be because he had not shown 'a clear intention to injure or provoke the descendants to such an extent that a serious breach of the peace ensued', as Judge Stephen himself had said would be necessary in a later clarification of his ruling of 1887. One of the clearest expositions of what is obviously 'Regina v. Ensor' is made in Winston Graham's novel *The Tumbled House* (1959).

Indeed, no case of criminal libel on the dead has succeeded in this century in view of this precedent, which was examined as late as 1975 by the Lord Chancellor's Committee on Defamation, chaired by Mr Justice Faulks. Although recommending a limited relaxation of the law as it stands regarding civil actions for libel of the dead, the report does not appear to recommend any change with regard to prosecution for criminal libel in this sphere.

In spite of several attempts to remove it, John Batchelor's statue still stands in the Hayes, looking towards the Docks which were the source of both pride and pain for him, and now it has been placed on the list of protected buildings and monuments.

Thornhill Crematorium, under the peaceful green slopes of Caerphilly Mountain, now provides for almost 3,000 cremations a year.

These are the two permanent memorials of the legal precedents set in Cardiff over ninety years ago, in the Old Town Hall Assize Court in St Mary Street—where the Commercial Bank of Wales now stands—by a truly distinguished, but tragic, judge.

'There are still good seats to be obtained'

The Life and Times of the Cardiff New Theatre: 1906-1977

by Peter Arnold

THE PROLOGUE—*Enter a Fire Engine*
One hundred years ago precisely, Cardiff lost its first and only purpose-built theatre. It wasn't a great conflagration, as these things go, although to people not brought up on disaster films and re-runs of footage from the Second World War, no doubt it was spectacular enough.

The old Theatre Royal had graced the site now occupied by the Park Hotel for exactly 50 years, and its fiery end was a sad blow to every citizen of Cardiff and its environs who enjoyed a visit to the theatre.

There *were* other theatres in the city—converted halls, and the like, but nothing which could really stand comparison with the genuine purpose-built article. It took 29 years to replace it.

Not that the Theatre Royal was quite dead. A footnote to the press advertisement announcing the inaugural season of the New Theatre in 1906, states that the owner and manager, Mr Robert Redford, was also the proprietor of the Theatre Royal, Cardiff, which that week was staging a production of 'The Freedom of Suzanne', with Miss Mabel Love and Mr Percy Hutchison. An ominous line stated that this was 'the last Engagement of Season at this Theatre'.

The time was to come when the Cardiff New Theatre became a mere footnote to the programmes of other theatres, but no one could possibly have foreseen that on 18 December 1906.

ACT ONE—*Beginners please*
The New Theatre was the pride of Robert Redford's life. It must have given him considerable pleasure to see his new purpose-built building rising, if not exactly from the ashes of the old Theatre Royal, then at least, only a few yards away, just across Park Place.

Robert Redford (no relation to the Sundance Kid, as far as we know) certainly knew what he was about. He engaged two of the best-known theatre builders of the day to design and construct his new venture, and appears to have given them a free hand to exercise their art.

Messrs Runtz and Ford were described in the Press as 'specialists in the planning of places of amusement', a claim they could undoubtedly justify. They had designed and built the Adelphi Theatre in London's West End, and also an intriguing complex called 'The New Gaiety Theatre and Restaurant', which seems to have had a vogue as a fashionable watering-place. Certainly, the Cardiff New Theatre was widely admired by patrons and artistes alike, and it is only in comparatively recent years that anything like major reconstruction has been necessary. Redford's other great coup was to secure the services of no less a personage than H. Beerbohm Tree, with his company, for the inaugural week.

Looking back from a distance of seven decades, we can only have a dim idea of the interest which the opening of the New Theatre must have aroused. Remember, there was no television, and the cinema was in its infancy. In any case, if you were a Nice Girl you didn't go to moving pictures —it meant sitting in the dark, which according to one commentator was an 'incentive to vice'. So, if you wanted to see the great actors of the time, you just had to visit the theatre. The opening of a spanking, new, ultra-modern one, must therefore have been a tremendous event for Cardiff.

Runtz and Ford did Cardiff proud. A contemporary description of the building is worth quoting at length:

NEW THEATRE,

PARK PLACE, CARDIFF,

SOLE PROPRIETOR AND MANAGER ... .. Mr. ROBERT REDFORD.

THE INAUGURAL WEEK

Commencing MONDAY, DECEMBER 10th, 1906,

FOR SIX NIGHTS, AND

Two Matinees Wednesday and Saturday, December 12th and 15th, at 2.15.

Mr. H. BEERBOHM TREE

AND HIS MAJESTY'S THEATRE COMPANY.

Western Mail, Limited, Cardiff.

Cover of the Inaugural Programme

The Building is of brick and Bath Stone. Seating accommodation is for 1,570. Principal Elevation is to the South East; the lower portion around the chief entrance is of Bath Stone . . . The top of this elevation is surmounted by two towers, which are utilised for ventilation purposes, and rise in height to nearly 50 feet above the pavement . . . The design of the whole is a free treatment of English Renaissance . . . Inside, both the corridor and staircase are richly carpeted, and are draped at the entrance; brass handrails being fixed at the sides. Each Portion of the House is provided with a spacious Saloon Bar; these for the Dress Circle and Orchestra Stalls being handsomely furnished and decorated. In this connection, special mention should be made of that for the Dress Circle, which is immediately over the Crush Room, and which, like it, is circular. The mural decorations for this, which are cream and gold, are extremely tasteful. The Dress Circle, Orchestra Stalls and Balcony are all furnished with tip-up seats, luxuriously upholstered in Crimson velvet. The seats in the Pit are upholstered in what is known as 'Railway Rep'.

After this, the commentator goes on at length about tasteful decorations, and concludes:

The Stage is one of the largest in the country, being no less than 76 feet in width and 54 feet in depth, while the height of the stage to the grid where the pulleys work is 57 feet. In only three or four of the very finest London theatres is there a larger stage, and that in Cardiff is second to none in the country in point of efficiency . . . The 17 dressing rooms, all are fitted with hot and cold water, electric light, gas etc.

Obviously, one Gentleman of the Press was sold on the place. We particularly like the way he made a bee-line for the bar before visiting the Auditorium. Plus ça change . . .

On 8 December 1906, the following notice appeared in the *Cardiff Times and South Wales Weekly News*:

NEW THEATRE, PARK PLACE, CARDIFF
Sole Proprietor and Manager—Robert Redford

Inaugural Week Commencing Mon. Dec. 10th, 1906

MR H. BEERBOHM TREE AND HIS MAJESTY'S THEATRE COMPANY

Monday and Thursday Evenings and Saturday Matinee
"TWELFTH NIGHT"

Tuesday and Saturday Evenings
"TRILBY" and "THE MAN WHO WAS"

Wednesday Matinee and Friday Evening
"COLONEL NEWCOME"

Wednesday Evening
"HAMLET"

Reserved Seats (Opening Night)—Boxes: £3.3s, £2.2s, £1.11s.6d. Dress Circle and Orchestra Stalls: 10s.6d. Balcony: 5s. Subsequent Performances—Boxes: £2.2s, £1.11s.6d, £1.1s. Dress Circle: 7s.6d. Orchestra Stalls: 6s. Pit Stalls: 5s. Balcony: 4s.

SPECIAL NOTICE: There are still good seats to be obtained for all performances.

Notably, Mr Redford did not feel it necessary to quote the times of any of these performances in his advertisement, although he was meticulous on the point when advertising his productions at the Theatre Royal. Perhaps interest was so great that patrons were willing to turn up early and wait for hours if necessary. In which case, the note about seats being available at all performances, coming as it did only two days before his gala opening, is a little mysterious.

Be that as it may, the New Theatre's first night was a triumph. The press reported:

The triumph achieved at the opening of Cardiff's New Theatre on Monday Night deserves to rank with the greatest. [The reporter also notes that there wasn't a vacant seat in the house, which makes Mr Redford's 'Special

Notice' even less explicable].

The social aspect of the occasion was no less triumphant than the theatrical one:

There were pretty faces everywhere, and there were almost as many pretty dresses. One saw gowns of ivory silk, shot with gold or silver threads; charming Empire frocks of cream and white satin, embroidered with trails of purple clematis and leaves. One sun-ray pleated shaded brown chiffon frock had a cloud of pale blue tulle round the shoulders, with here and there, a few Gloire de Dijon Roses. There were also lovely dresses of green and faintest pink. The scene, like the programme and performance, was a memorable one.

Indeed, it must have been. With Beerbohm Tree playing Malvolio to Constance Collier's Olivia, in the newest, most modern theatre in the whole of Edwardian Great Britain; with the Boer War over and the Great War almost eight years away; with Britannia ruling the waves, and a turn-of-the-century Welsh Christmas only two weeks away . . . they don't make first nights like that any more.

The cast took five curtain calls, after which Beerbohm Tree was prevailed upon to speak; which he did, at some length.

It was a great source of pride to me as an Actor, when I cast my eyes on this building and its surroundings, to know that in your beautiful Park, where you have already your Municipal Buildings and your Law Courts; where you have also your University College and your National Museum, that you have been able to find a place for a Theatre. (applause)—showing that in Cardiff you regard a Theatre, not only as a place of amusement, but as a means of Education (applause).

He also consoled his audience for not being able to claim Shakespeare as a Welshman, adding that the Bard did not belong to any one country, but 'to every province in the whole World'. So there.

After Tree's flow of well-meant oratory dried up, the audience shouted for 'Redford', who was eventually found and led forward by Tree himself. Mr Redford seems to have been genuinely affected by the enthusiasm and warmth of his first-night audience. After thanking them for their 'kind reception and attendance', he promised: 'If the public rally round me in the future, I will give them the best the stage can produce'. And he did his level best to do just that.

ACT TWO—'How much better fare'

It didn't take Redford long to score another smashing success—and while he was doing it, he established a tradition which still persists at the 'New' and constitutes one of the great highlights of every year. To quote the *Western Mail* of 27 December 1906: 'No longer need South Walians go so far as Bristol to see a brilliant Pantomime'.

Redford's choice for the Cardiff New Theatre's first panto was 'Red Riding Hood'. It was a joint production with Milton Bode, and the book was specially written for the New Theatre by J. Hackery Wood. A strong cast included Ainsley Burton, Annie Purcell and Ted and Mary Hopkins.

The show opened on Boxing day, and was enthusiastically received by both press and audiences. It was certainly a lavish production, even by the more spacious standards of the day. The final scene was a real stunner, with the jingoistic overtones which were almost obligatory at the time. Wrote the *Mail*:

The final scene, 'The King's Pageant', is symbolic of the four countries of the British Isles. When the curtain rose it showed an exceedingly pretty scene in which the Prince of Wales Feathers was the principal subject, and ladies dressed in the symbolism of Wales appeared. The scene disappeared and disclosed a beautiful network of purple thistles, which was followed by a delicate screen of shamrock. Finally, when the whole scene was disclosed one saw steps leading to a huge crystal globe set in a bower of roses, on which stood Britannia with an illuminated shield.

Stirring stuff.

Other press commentators were equally enthusiastic, although one observed, 'If it had a weakness, it was in the absence of smart local allusions, but this is a defect not too late to remedy'.

Perhaps that critic was feeling a trifle liverish that night, because, while allowing that Ainsley Burton as Marmaduke, 'the unprincipled old squire', did a lot of good work, he also remarks that the actor's voice 'did not carry to all parts of the Theatre'. The *Western Mail* had the last word however, commenting that Robert Redford had 'given his Patrons an early opportunity to judge how much better fare he means to provide for them at his new property'.

Indeed, 1907 was a busy year for Redford and his New Theatre. In February, George Dance brought 'The Beauty of Bath' from Hicks'

It's doubtful if the Cardiff New Theatre has ever seen more activity than it has over the last couple of years. Houses now comfortably top the 500 mark annually. That's ten a *week*!

Theatre, London, and returned in March with 'The Little Michus' described as a comic opera. Also in March, another New Theatre tradition was established—allowing local amateur companies the use of the theatre. From 4-6 March, Cardiff Operatic Society staged 'The Yeoman of the Guard'.

Altogether the production list for 1907 reads like a catalogue of Edwardian drama—'The Sign of the Cross', 'The Catch of the Season', 'The Geisha', 'Floradora' and many others, often with the leading performers of the day much in evidence.

In May, Charles Cartwright brought David Copperfield for just one night. It did such good business that he brought it back again in September. In June, Seymour Hicks and Zena Dare starred in 'Scrooge', which seems an odd time of the year for it. George Alexander's company gave Pinero's 'His House in Order' in September, closely followed by Mrs Patrick Campbell in 'The Second Mrs Tanqueray'.

The Carl Rosa Opera sang 'Il Trovatore', 'Lohengrin' and 'Carmen' in October, while the D'Oyly Carte gave 'Mikado' and 'Gondoliers'. And in November, Beerbohm Tree was back for a whole week, with a repertoire which included a world premiere of an adaptation of Dickens' 'Mystery of Edwin Drood'.

The year closed with a pantomime, of course; 'Jack the Giant Killer' this time. The interesting thing is that the theatre didn't close for rehearsals until 21 December, with the traditional Boxing Day opening. That would seem to argue a busy Christmas for everyone concerned.

1908 was much the same. A continual procession of the greatest in the theatre, and the most talked-about productions. It may seem churlish to gloss over such performers as Marie Studholm, Pauline Chase, Martin Harvey and William Mollison, but pride of place must go to a single Wednesday Matinee, on 17 June. The *Western Mail* again:

A Franco-Welsh welcome is awaiting MADAME SARAH BERNHARDT on her brief visit to Cardiff today. In the green room before the performance, the popular actress will be presented with an elegantly designed little memento by the Société Anglo-Française.

For her single visit to Cardiff, for one performance only, and that in the afternoon, Sarah Bernhardt had elected to give her most famous role—'La Dame aux Camelias'. She could hardly have chosen anything else.

The *Western Mail* was somewhat overawed by the occasion. The 18 June edition carried these headlines:

MADAME BERNHARDT IN CARDIFF
'LA DAME AUX CAMELIAS' PRODUCED
THE PATHOS OF WONDERFUL ACTING
If it were not an impertinence to do so in the case of an actress like Madame Bernhardt, we might say that she achieved a great success in Cardiff on Wednesday. It was the quick passage of a meteor, but it had all the meteor's brilliance and glory. A matinee performance was all the greatest tragedienne of the age could spare us; nevertheless the New Theatre was crammed.

No audience could have been more appreciative. This last is all the more noteworthy, because the play selected was in French.

The superlatives continue, but for our purposes, the point is that 'The Divine Sarah's' performance at the New Theatre was the ultimate accolade, beside which the arrival of Henry Irving in 'The Bells' is anticlimactic.

There was no doubt—the Cardiff New Theatre had arrived.

ACT THREE—*'Fin de siecle'*

Nothing could stop the New Theatre now. It almost seemed as though everyone who was anyone in the theatre was jostling to play 'The New'. Beerbohm Tree became a regular visitor, as did the Carl Rosa and D'Oyly Carte. George Edwardes and Charles Frohman between them staged a long series of musical comedies which included just about all the legendary greats— 'Waltz Dream', 'Merry Widow', 'Floradora' (again), 'The Dollar Princess' and all the rest. In fact, most of them, particularly 'Merry Widow' and 'The Belle of New York' came back again and again.

In 1912 came another great coup. No less a personage than Anna Pavlova herself danced at the New Theatre with members of the Imperial Russian Ballet. They were so impressed by the facilities accorded them, and the reception they received, that they returned in December of the same year.

The critics came too. At least, George Bernard Shaw did. The reason for his visit was to attend the farewell performance of the great Forbes Robertson, who was presenting 'Hamlet' in Cardiff. His 'critical essay' on Robertson runs to thousands of words. Perhaps the most Shavian passage in the whole piece remarks 'To call Hamlet mad because he did not anticipate Schopenhauer, is like calling Marcellus mad because he did not refer the ghost to the Psychical Research Society'. Which is good Shaw, but doesn't really tell us much about the occasion, 65 years later.

What Shaw would have thought of the Drury Lane production of Ben Hur which visited the New Theatre in March 1913 is anyone's guess. The advance publicity tells us that it 'Includes the Great Chariot Race. Colossal Cast of 100 Artistes. 15 Horses, Camels Etc.'.

But another colossal event was waiting in the wings; one which was to change everything for everyone. Not that the New Theatre seemed to take much notice. On the very day that the Great War began, Hall Caine's great play 'The Christian' was playing to packed houses.

Business went on as usual. Pantomimes were as lavish and well-supported as ever. The great and famous brought their productions as regularly as they had ever done. In 1917 one significant event did take place. The Cardiff New Theatre showed a film. Admittedly it was the greatest blockbuster of its time—D. W. Griffith's epic 'Birth of a Nation', but, with hindsight, it was rather like inviting a burglar in to inspect the family silver.

The War did change the theatre however. The flapper age, according to contemporary observers, brought a dearth of good new plays. Slowly and subtly, the fare at the New Theatre began to change—and not always for the better. Certainly, 'The New' was usually able to produce good Shakespearean productions, and the like, but by 1926, Hamilton Deane's 'Dracula' and Murray Carrington's 'White Cargo' were more typical of the offerings at the theatre, than was anything else offered that year.

The big event of 1929 seems to have been 'The Wireless Favourites' starring Flotsam and

Anna Pavlova in 'Le Cygne' (The Passing of a Swan) by Saint-Saëns

Anna Pavlova. Illustration taken from the brochure
produced for her visit to the New Theatre

Jetsam—good stuff, certainly, but hardly Bernhardt, Pavlova or Tree.

By 1936 The Cardiff New Theatre was, frankly,
a twice-nightly variety theatre. Nat Gonella,
Hetty King, Harry Roy, Claude Dampier—they
all came. And they were all greats in their way.
Unfortunately, not even that could be said for
much longer.

A random selection of offerings from 1940
speaks for itself, only too clearly. Phyllis Dixie
(who even cut her famous fan dance from the
programme), Carroll Levis and his Discoveries,
'We're in the Army Now', 'Gaieties de Mont-
martre' and—would you believe—'Naughty Girls
of 1940'!

The decline of a once-great institution is an
unedifying spectacle at best, and we make no
apology for glossing over the next two decades,
with their 'Jane of the Daily Mirrors', their
'look-alike' shows—where artistes got a job solely
on the strength of a resemblance to famous

performers—and the nude shows rendered im-
mobile by the Lord Chamberlain.

Cinema did its work. So did Television. Crowds
went away, the building became dilapidated.
Redford's brilliant conception became, in essence,
a theatrical whore. And it wasn't alone. All over
the country theatres were closing. The natural
resilience of the New Theatre, in fact, enabled it
to last longer than any other Cardiff theatre. But
it couldn't go on. In 1962 the owners, Stoll
Theatres, had had enough, and called a halt.

ACT FOUR—'Into the breach dear friends'

In the end it was one word 'Bingo' which started
the rebirth of the Cardiff New Theatre. The idea
that the cry of 'legs eleven' might echo from the
stage which Pavlova herself had graced, was too
much for Cardiff. That, and the fact that the
'New' was the last live theatre in the Capital of
the Principality, spurred many and diverse people
into action.

An active pressure group called the 'Cardiff
New Theatre Society' made its presence felt in no
uncertain terms. The Cardiff City Council moved
quickly to make a Preservation of Use Order,
which forbade any use for the Theatre other than
for theatrical purposes. The Welsh Arts Council
gave their support.

Stoll Theatres were in something of a cleft
stick. They couldn't use the theatre as anything
but a theatre, and they couldn't afford to use the
building *as* a theatre. The breathing space provided
by the Preservation of Use Order was used to
great advantage.

By August 1963 the City Council had taken the
lead in forming the New Theatre Trust, and had
negotiated a lease of the building with Stoll
Theatres.

The Trust was composed in the ratio of 75%
members of the local authority (who were, after
all, putting up most of the money), and 25%
other interested parties, including the Welsh Arts
Council, BBC, HTV, University of Wales and,
of course, the Cardiff New Theatre Society. The

Articles of Association also provide that the Secretary of the Trust be the Chief Executive of the Council, and that the Treasurer should be the City Treasurer. In fact, it is obvious that all concerned meant business from the very first.

The Arts Council donated £6,000 to get the project off the ground. The City Council's contribution was nearer £15,000. In the first half-year of operation—from August 1963 to April 1964, 204 performances were staged at the revitalised New Theatre. 205,000 people saw the productions, and £75,400 was taken at the box office. In the first full year—1964/5—the number of houses went up to 398, patrons numbered

The impressive interior of the New Theatre

326,000 and takings rose to £123,000.

While not breaking any theatrical records, the first three years of leasing the theatre were a success, although subsidy from Council and Arts Council was still necessary, as it still is. The Local Authority had no hesitation in renewing the lease for another three years.

But all was not plain sailing. A succession of management problems didn't do the theatre any good at all, and weren't cured until 1969, when Martin Williams, took over as Administrator.*

To the Local Authority's great credit, they never flinched, and in 1969 took the far-seeing step of actually purchasing the theatre, so that the future of theatre in Cardiff is no longer purely in the hands of commercial and economic forces.

In 1970 to 1971, the Municipal Authorities didn't need to subsidise the theatre at all, a happy position which has, so far, not arisen again, although this is partly accounted for by the extensive renovation and development which has taken place in Runtz and Ford's fine building since then.

One crucial decision was taken over this period. No longer does the Cardiff New Theatre have to arrange productions on the basis of making a good commercial deal. Nowadays, the Trust and the theatre management pursue a policy of excellence, to the great good fortune of Cardiff and all South Wales.

This has meant that, for the first time since the theatre's palmy days, 'The New' can stage its own productions. This means original pantomimes, for example, but it also means ambitious and praiseworthy efforts such as the 1976 production of 'Toad of Toad Hall', which the late Martin Williams, who directed the production himself, claimed was the first really full-scale version of the piece for many years; certainly it was the only production which matched A. A. Milne's original concept within living memory.

When the current economic crisis hit us, things didn't look good for the New Theatre, or for any other similar establishment for that matter. It would have been simple to reduce staff, cut performances, create a siege economy and generally try to sit the situation out.

But that's not the way at 'The New' these days. The other alternative was to increase productivity and profitability. It's doubtful if the Cardiff New Theatre has ever seen more activity than it has over the last couple of years. Houses now annually top the 500 mark comfortably. That's ten a *week*!

Things happen in the mornings, afternoons and evenings—including special performances for schools, late night film shows, lunchtime jazz sessions. In the eight weeks of the 1976/7 pantomime (starring Stan Stennett for the third year—with a fourth booked for 1977) no less than 100,000 people passed the box office.

The future for 'The New' is bright. We may never see the time when a single-auditorium, mixed-performance theatre can be a commercially successful venture again, but there are other considerations, linked to the quality of life, to the cultural life of a community, and to the provision of opportunity to artistes, writers, musicians—and for that matter, playgoers. As long as Cardiff has an enlightened local authority, and as long as the public of South Wales and beyond demonstrates by its support that a theatre like 'The New' has an important function to fulfill, these other considerations are in safe hands.

Much more could be written about the Cardiff New Theatre. Insufficient credit has been given, for example, to the New Theatre Society, which does such sterling service for the theatre, and for the performing arts in Cardiff generally.

And, of course, the surface has hardly been scratched when it comes to recording the great performers who have graced the stage in Park Place—better than ever since rebuilding in 1976. However, Robert Redford's first 'Special Notice' is as true now as it was in 1906. There *are* good seats to be obtained at all performances!

---

*Sad to record Martin Williams died at the tragically early age of 32 while this book was in course of production.

49

Cardiff City Fire Brigade

A brief history by M. J. Mace

AN EFFICIENT FIRE fighting service, on call 24 hours a day, every day of the year, is today taken for granted, but as the history of the Cardiff Fire Service shows, it is a very recent phenomenon.

This is not to say that many hundreds of years ago, men did not band themselves together to fight a fire. In the very early days of the Roman Empire, the Romans at first relied upon a series of private fire brigades, and later the Emperor set up a corps of Vigiles. In Britain, rather surprisingly in view of the toll which fire has always claimed in terms of life, goods and property, it was only after a long struggle that fire fighters obtained sufficient recognition to warrant the creation of a 'Fire Department' within the framework of local government.

The growth of the Fire Service in Britain can be traced from the Great Fire of London in 1666, through the era of insurance company control to 1847 when provision of a paid fire brigade was made lawful, but not compulsory. Not until 1938 was this legal step taken to ensure adequate fire protection for the public. In 1941 came 'nationalisation' and with the post-war years the present structure of local authority fire service was born.

The Cardiff Fire Service of today is a far cry from that of yesteryear; the self-propelled modern pump water tender has replaced the manuals and horsedrawn 'steamers' of the old days and a devotion to diesel or petrol engines has replaced the fireman's traditional love of the horse, but the spirit of the Service still remains. A fireman of today is a fully trained, uniformed member of a public force, always ready for action and service.

The Early Days

To go back to the beginning, it was in 1836 that mention is first made in the *Cardiff Records* of fire protection of the borough. Before that there appeared to be no organised police force or anyone responsible for the supervision of any fire protection arrangements. However, parochial records from St John the Baptist Church show that as far back as 1739 a manual fire engine was kept in the porch of the church tower for use by the parish for fire fighting and that a bell in the tower was rung to warn the inhabitants of a fire. This parochial initiative is not surprising, for the church in those days was the focus of community life.

The parish was very proud of its fire engine for which the church sexton was responsible and these entries show that money was spent to keep the engine and its equipment efficient:-

1739 A/c of Henry Llewellyn and Alexander Purcell—Churchwardens 'To William Thomas for ale for playing the engine' 2/6d.

1771 The churchwardens examined the bills at a vestry meeting on 4th March rendered by David Pritchard Carpenter, and Thomas Richard Smith for the repairs to the fire engine, which amounted to £5.15s.0d. The vestry decided that the work was only worth £4.4s.0d. and after a vote agreed to pay them that amount.

1881 A vestry meeting decided 'that the fire engine be repaired, and that the Church Wardens do purchase a new engine, pipes, and buckets, which is on sale from the Lady Blosse of Gabalva'.

The first fire escape was purchased in 1853 and in August 1867 the efficiency of the steam engine and fire escape was tested before the Corporation Officials who were satisfied with the performance of the appliances and the agility of the members of the fire brigade in getting to work with the escape.

At that time, the fire warning bell was still being rung at St John's Church and the *Cardiff Chron-*

icle on 5 October, reporting a serious fire in a bonded store at the top of the west dock, added 'information was at once sent to the fire engine station and a fireman afterwards sent to the Royal Hotel for the horses and at once began to get steam up. The Fire Bell at St John's Church was rung . . .'

By now the population of Cardiff was about 35,000 and there were 32 miles of streets, with the development of Splott, Roath, Grangetown and Canton just starting. The Bute East Dock had been built and the old river bed filled in. The water main supply had been increased and extra reservoirs built at Llandaff and Llanishen but although mains now served a number of major streets, those in between had no mains water supply. Obviously there were few hydrants attached to the mains for fire fighting and this had become painfully obvious

to the Town Council for in 1868 a committee was set up to look into the matter of providing a proper water supply in case of fire.

The passing of the Cardiff Improvement Act in 1875 generated still further growth of Cardiff and made fire fighting even more important. At this time the fire brigade was run on a voluntary, part-time basis but in 1878 the brigade became a 'Police Brigade'. This followed a submission by Walter Hemmingway, the Superintendent of the Police and Fire Brigade, that the fire brigade, as constituted, be abolished and a 'Police Fire Brigade' organised.

The Brigade was to be as follows:-

12 Police Constables to do police and fire duty, the police purposes being met by these constables performing reserve patrols or duty upon home beats, or near the fire engine

Cardiff Fire Brigade, 1874, photographed in the Town Hall Yard
Photograph courtesy Cardiff Central Library

station, equally dividing and extending over the 24 hours.

This would, Hemmingway estimated, ensure the mustering of six men in four or five minutes and in one minute a reel and hose could be despatched followed by the steam engine. These constables would be paid an extra two shillings a week for performing this duty, and in addition, there were the engineer and his deputy who did whole time fire duty. Cardiff, in accepting Hemmingway's recommendations for a 'Police Fire Brigade' was following the example set in Liverpool, Birkenhead, Rochdale and Wigan.

Although no doubt grateful for the protection the firemen gave, the public were not slow in pointing a finger at them. Typical of this attitude was a complaint by the Rev. G. A. Jones of the Temperance Town School Chapel that at between 6 and 7a.m. on 8 March 1880, windows were broken and the chapel deluged with water while the brigade was practising. This was denied by the Head Constable who said the windows were broken before the day in question.

In 1880 the purchase of the new horse-drawn steam fire engine was hotly debated at a Watch Committee meeting. The old engine, with a capacity of 300 gallons per minute, needed repair and the debate was whether to repair it or buy a new one. On 5 June 1880 a steam fire engine, manufactured by Merryweather and Sons Limited, was given a test on the canal bank, North Road, before members of the Watch Committee with Mr Merryweather present. This engine, with reciprocating pump, was between 60 and 70 h.p. and 120 strokes per minute, and running at a moderate speed, could deliver 720 g.p.m.

The main argument against buying a new steam engine like the model demonstrated was that often there was not even enough water to supply the pumping capacity of the old engine so that to buy a new engine with a larger capacity seemed, to some members of the Committee, to be a waste of money. Hemmingway's answer was that more lines of hose could be got

to work from the new model than from the old model and that at the recent test at the canal, six jets were operating from the appliance, throwing water 100ft and one jet even threw water 220ft high. He also reminded the Watch Committee that the old engine could not supply sufficient pressure to play jets onto the top of high buildings such as Howells in St Mary Street in sufficient quantity.

The old steam fire engine did not couple up direct to hydrants as can be done by modern appliances. A dam, or 'cistern' as it was termed in those days, was carried and if open water was not available this 'cistern' was filled from the nearest hydrant and the suction of the steamer set into the dam. The water supply for fire fighting was still poor at this time. In all there were only 15 fire plugs, with a diameter a mere 1¼", attached to the mains.

A meeting at last resolved to buy the new steam fire engine for £822 from Merryweathers with the old engine traded in as part exchange. They also resolved to go into the matter of increasing the supply of water for fire fighting and enlarging the diameter of the fire plugs. It was believed that now the Corporation had the Water Works under their control and had already succeeded in obtaining powers to increase the water supply to the city, within five years sufficient water would be laid on to supply the new engine, grandiosely named 'the Fire Queen'.

Another important date was Wednesday 25 August 1880, when the Cardiff Fire Brigade were issued with their first brass helmets and a new uniform.

The turn of the century saw the plans for a new town hall and law courts approved by the Secretary of State, starting a train of events which led to the provision of Cardiff's magnificent civic centre. Throughout 1900 argument raged over the purchase of land which was 'urgently required for fire brigade purposes'. This was to foreshadow the fine new headquarters to be built later at Westgate Street/Quay Street. At the Watch Committee meeting on 13 June 1900 the Borough Engineer was instructed to prepare plans for the proposed new station and when submitted on 11 December 1901 his estimate for the work was £15,250.

There was disagreement over the siting of the proposed new fire station. The Head Constable recommended to the Watch Committee in 1904 that it should be built in Cathays Park and the Town Hall Committee was requested to assign a site as near as possible to the police station, but the Committee postponed consideration of the matter. Six years later the City Engineer produced revised plans and estimates for the new 'Chief Fire Brigade Station' at Westgate Street,

and also, under a proposed decentralisation scheme, for two subsidiary Fire Stations, one at Beresford Road Bridge to serve Roath and the other on the corner of Wellington Street and the new Kitchener Road to cover Canton. The revised estimate for the Central Station was now £54,466. 5s.7d. and for each of the subsidiary stations £5,666.3s.9d.

The Head Constable still doubted whether the Westgate Street site could provide the essentials although he conceded that the subsidiary stations would temporarily reduce the objections to Westgate Street from the point of view of accommodation. He claimed that, as the city grew, it would

Cardiff Fire Station, 1890
Photograph by permission of National Museum of Wales

also increase in importance at its centre, particularly in the improvement of its public buildings, business houses and places of public amusement and that the equipment and staff would have to be substantially increased from time to time at the Central Station to cope with all the demands. He doubted whether there was enough space in Westgate Street for such enlargement.

A scheme of decentralisation was recommended with subsidiary stations situated in the east and west end of the city, and the reduction of accommodation at the new Central Fire Station to an engine room for two steamers and one motor fire escape plus two 'reels'. The engine room was completely equipped on the most up-to-date lines with automatic quick opening doors, suspending gear for harness, polished steel descent poles and telephonic call apparatus. Living accommodation was reduced to single men's quarters for six men, superintendents, first and second engineer's quarters and accommodation for eight married men with families.

The new fire station in Westgate Street, which was opened in 1917, did great credit to the wisdom and foresight of the Council and its officials in the eventual selection of the site, in the very heart of the city and yet sufficiently distant in those days from congested streets to enable the brigade to make 'a flying start' at any moment of the day or night.

The lofty and imposing six-storey building, of brick and concrete in Georgian style with portland stone dressings, was considered one of the finest elevations of its kind in the country. Covering 5,600 sq. ft. it had a frontage to Westgate Street of 140ft and with its fine range of folding engine exit doors, its picturesque tiled roof, surmounted by a well designed tower overlooking the famous Cardiff Arms Park, was a striking example of what can be done to combine

'The King' Merryweather steam fire engine in Cathays Park, June 1906

54

aesthetic lines with utilitarian requirements. There was a spacious yard at the rear of the premises—the 'wings' were not added until 1928—a specially constructed drill tower, hose drying tower, deep lift testing well and an up-to-date workshop.

When the station was opened it was thought that the main appliance room, which housed eight machines, would provide adequate accommodation for all the engines and special appliances that would be needed for many years, but by the 1930s the capacity of the station was becoming overstrained. It was not just a case of merely containing all the engines, escapes and other equipment, but of positioning them so that any one of them could be driven out of the station within seconds.

The living accommodation on the upper floors was sufficient to provide 28 comfortable quarters with laundry, reading room and offices for the firemen, there being separate living rooms for the superintendent and other officers, but by 1928 the problem of overcrowding was acute.

1919: The Police Fire Brigade

In 1918 there appeared to be a unique opportunity for fully incorporating the brigade into the police force and this was the authority's obvious intention. Owing to vacancies and the mobilisation of H.M. Forces, police had had to be attached to the brigade to maintain it at a reasonable working standard and other factors had led to the brigade, as a whole, being placed on practically the same basis as the police in relation to pay, bonus and pensions. Conversion of the firemen to policemen therefore presented no insuperable difficulties. Consequently, the Watch Committee in January 1918 advocated the full incorporation of the brigade into the police force and resolved that a superintendent be appointed, the post to be advertised at a salary of £221 per year rising to a maximum of £260 (it was eventually advertised at £400 p.a. rising to £460 in four years). It was also proposed that the fire brigade be reorganised and increased in personnel although it was expected that any increase would

Superintendent G. Geen in the Old Station Yard with 'steamers' 1913

probably have to be postponed until men were available. The amalgamation finally took place at the end of 1919.

Most of the brigade's equipment was rapidly becoming obsolete, mainly due to the war, and it was clear that the two 'steamers' would not last much longer. By June 1918 another motor fire engine was on order from Leyland, together with a turn-table fire escape. The motor engine was 40/60 h.p. with 500 g.p.m. pump and carrying an escape ladder (£1,550). The 80ft turn-table ladder, operated by compressed air and self propelled, cost £1,050. The boiler of the old 'William McKenzie' eventually failed and attempts were made to sell the steamer since repairs were not

The Appliance Room in Westgate Street Station, 1917

economical. It eventually realised £100 and a buyer was at last found for the old, 'swinging harness' which raised £12.10s.

Problems caused by increasing motor traffic in the city were relieved when the new orbital road—Western Avenue—was opened on 11 July 1933. There were many serious fires in Cardiff between the wars, one of which occurred at the premises of Cross Brothers on 20 December 1935 when the skill and courage of the brigade prevented the blaze spreading to adjoining valuable properties. There was high praise from James Howell and Company who showed their appreciation with donations to the Widows and Orphans Fund.

Another spectacular fire, on 18 January 1937, destroyed the grandstand of Cardiff City AFC at Ninian Park, while a month later, in a serious fire at the Cymric Buildings, West Bute Street, members of the brigade displayed remarkable promptitude and coolness and Superintendent Bainbridge and Sergeant Collins were instrumental in saving three children from a bedroom using a life-line. The Superintendent and Sergeant later received the silver and bronze medals of the Society for the Protection of Life from Fire.

1938: The AFS

The idea of a part-time Auxiliary Fire Brigade was born in April 1937 when the government were becoming increasingly concerned with the need for air-raid precaution. It was first suggested that the use of police as auxiliary firemen should be dispensed with, but this suggestion was rejected by a London Conference which claimed that the existing method of fire brigade organ-

A serious fire at the premises of Cross Brothers, 20 December 1935

isation was both sound and economical. It was felt that reserves for emergency purposes such as air-raid precautions should be recruited from the public and paid for by the state.

Press adverts appeared inviting citizens aged 25 to 50 to enrol as volunteer special constables and auxiliary firemen to assist the police and fire brigade to safeguard the civilian population in the event of attack by enemy aircraft. Auxiliary firemen were medically examined and underwent a course of special training—they were to be paid for their services only in any actual emergency, but received a 'bonus' of £1 at the end of training. Suitable citizens were also enrolled at this time as 'air-raid wardens' and they also received limited instruction in fire brigade work.

By the end of 1937, 85 auxiliary firemen out of a required total for Cardiff of 200 had been enrolled in response to the advertisement and emergency fire fighting equipment was supplied by the government. The basis of duty of the Cardiff AFS was similar to that of the regular Brigade, the three platoon system—8 hours duty,

8 hours liberty, 8 hours stand-by with one leave day per week, when practicable. When necessary tours of actual duty could be extended to 12 hours per day. Full-time personnel were required, under air-raid conditions, to give such hours of duty as were required by the service, which meant continuous duty working with stand-by according to local circumstances.

During the war, in which the AFS bore the brunt of the 'blitz', there were ordinary fires just as in peacetime. One incident occurred at 377 Cowbridge Road on 13 February 1941, at which great gallantry was displayed by Sergeant J. Germain and Police Fireman J. E. Harding of the Fire Brigade in rescuing two unconscious people. A Mr H. Griffiths assisted in the rescue before the arrival of the Fire Brigade and Mr A. Summers, Constable T. James, Fireman S. Thomas and Mr S. C. Gresham made strenuous efforts to assist the occupants of the house to safety. The Society for the Protection of Life from Fire awarded bronze medals to the Sergeant and Firemen and a framed certificate to Mr

Dennis pumping unit fitted with 35ft 'Ajax' ladder (400-800 g.p.m.). Supplied in 1935 at a cost of £1,355

58

The old Control Room at Westgate Street, 1953
Photograph courtesy Western Mail & Echo Ltd

Griffiths. This was an historic fire call in that it was the first time for use to be made of wireless transmission between a fire engine in Cardiff and the fire station. Considerable time was saved in calling an ambulance for the removal of the injured.

1941: National Fire Service

From 18 August 1941 full responsibility for the operation and administration of the Regular and Auxiliary Fire Services was transferred to the Secretary of State. During the transitional period, until the new organisation was established, existing Fire Authorities continued to exercise certain day to day functions in connection with the administration, but the cost of the new Fire Service

was in fact borne by the Exchequer from 1 July 1941, subject to an annual contribution by each Fire Authority of 75% of the cost of its regular fire brigade in the standard year 1939/40. Cardiff City Council placed on record their wholehearted admiration of the outstanding qualities of leadership displayed by Chief Constable Mr. J. A. Wilson, C.B.E., particularly during heavy attacks on the city, and tendered to all ranks of the Regular and Auxiliary Fire Brigades, its profound gratitude for the loyal service and high standard of efficiency.

So was born the National Fire Service and with its formation came the break in the links which had bound together the local police force and the fire brigade for so many years. At the end of the 'duration of the emergency' local authority was to get back its fire service and never again was it to be under police control.

1948: The New City Fire Station

The new Cardiff City Fire Service was controlled, for the Fire Authority, by the Watch Committee as also was the City Police Force. The first Chief Fire Officer was Mr W. Gayton, KPM, Grad.I.Fire E, who took up his duties on the 'appointed day', 1 April 1948.

One result following the nationalisation was that although even as far back as the early 1900s, help would be given by Cardiff in fighting fires in neighbouring urban and rural districts, neighbouring brigades were now required to help each other on request. This was freely given and received by the Glamorgan and Monmouthshire County Districts, and mutual assistance was also arranged between Cardiff and Newport.

During its formative years the new service was called upon to provide many 'special services' including rescuing cats from high buildings, removing horses and cows from culverts and receiving and transmitting urgent messages about serious road accidents. The equipment available and the training of service personnel made them particularly adept at performing these extra duties for the public. The advice of the newly formed Fire Prevention Department was increasingly sought by the public and local authority departments and many inspections were carried out. About 1,000 people a year visited the Central Fire Station during the first three years of the new service, many on visits arranged by city organisations. There was regular liaison at the time with staff of the Ministry of Civil Aviation Fire Training School at Pengam Airport and the loss of the valuable training expertise was keenly felt some years later when, upon industrial development of the site, the school was transferred to another part of the country.

Although plans were prepared as early as 1952 and sites earmarked for two district fire stations to cover the new developments to the west, north and east, and to provide ultimately more speedy fire cover, the economic situation delayed construction. Subsequently a new western station was provided at Cowbridge Road West, Ely, which with the Whitchurch Fire Station, transferred from Glamorgan County Council in 1966 following the extension of the city boundary, and a new station in Colchester Avenue, relieved very considerably the difficulties of 'backing up' from the Central Station due to heavy traffic congestion.

Several fire fatalities took place in 1953 and one particularly spectacular tragedy occurred at Llandaff where a woman lost her life when an aircraft crashed on to a private hotel. Other serious fires occured at the Oram Brush Company in John Street, Docks; Cardiff Waste Paper Company, Collingdon Road; and Curran Steels Limited in Curran Road. A Presbyterian Church and the Cardiff Technical College at Cathays Park were also severely damaged. In this year assistance was also sent to flooded areas of the east coast of Britain. The fire service in Cardiff was at this time attending about 70% more calls annually than in 1958 and it was difficult to account for the whole of this consistent increase. This seemingly worrying fact was deceptive as most senior fire officers believed that the increase in calls was not a matter of undue concern but rather an indication of the growing realisation by the public of the service so readily and freely available. One of the obvious results of these more frequent calls was that fires and suspicious circumstances connected with possible fire were quickly tackled, with minimal loss.

A fire occurred on Christmas Day 1955 at the headquarters building in Westgate Street, proving that the old enemy is capable of striking in the most unlikely places! Fire damage was confined to the large roof space over the residential flats in the building and the operational efficiency of the service was not affected, but considerable damage was caused by water to the quarters of the upper floors and the incident presented some difficult fire fighting problems.

The year 1958 was one of steady progress and

achievement. The total number of calls received was 1,226, a decrease of 67 from the previous year, probably due to a bad summer which cut the number of grass and associated fires. By far the most serious fire to have occurred in Cardiff for many years took place in the early hours of Saturday 16 August 1958, involving a large building used mainly as a warehouse of multiple occupancy in the city centre. The fire was a typical example of the results of late discovery and the building had become totally involved before it was discovered by the night-watchman

of an adjacent building. It took 17 jets from 8 pumps and 2 turn-table ladders to subdue the fire, at Nos. 13/19 The Hayes.

A landmark in the history of the Fire Service not only in Cardiff but in Britain was the setting up in 1971 by the Home Secretary of a Committee of Enquiry, to look into the work of the whole-time members of the Fire Service including control room staff in Great Britain and to advise on an evaluation of the work. Members of the Committee led by the Chairman, Sir Charles Cunningham C.B.E., accompanied by H.M.

The Hayes fire—'one of the most serious to have occurred in Cardiff for many years'—took place on 16 August 1958
Photograph courtesy Western Mail & Echo Ltd.

Westgate Street Station, demolished in 1973 to make way for a multi-storey car park

Headquarters Fire Control, 1977

The new Fire Service headquarters in Adamsdown

Chief Inspector of Fire Services, made a formal fact finding visit to the City Fire Service on 9 July 1971.

One particularly worrying fire occurred at the Esso Petroleum Company in Ferry Road, Grangetown, on 26 March 1971 when all work at the depot was suspended and a water curtain put up to cover the oil storage tanks nearest to the bitumen plant. The tank affected was eventually flooded with carbon dioxide, after arrival of a bulk supply. Another unusual fire occurred in September 1972 when flames swept through the MV *Cassarate*, a 15,000 ton cargo ship at Cardiff Dock. Thousands of gallons of water were pumped into the ship during the night and flames leapt 30ft high as timber and rubber blazed in the holds. Water flooded into a lower hold containing tapioca which began to swell and created a danger to the steel plating. The *Cassarate* soon became internationally famous as the news media dubbed it 'the tapioca time-bomb'.

In 1972 the annual total of incidents attended reached 4,574, the highest ever recorded and an interesting comparison with the statistics at the start of this story.

The final major development in the Cardiff City Fire Service was the provision of new headquarters, adjacent to Adam Street, providing easy access to all parts of the central area and to the remainder of the city. The new headquarters, officially opened in March 1973, consists of a four-storey block containing the control room, administrative offices and accommodation for duty crews, single-storey appliance room accommodating seven appliances and stores, workshop garages and smoke training centre grouped around a drill yard containing a 60ft high hose drying tower and deep lift well - 36ft deep - containing 8,000 gallons of water for pump testing purposes. The control room contains a console with positions for two operators and is equipped to monitor all incoming calls and alarms and to exercise direct control of all district stations and appliances.

The end of this story is in fact the beginning— the beginning of a new chapter in the story of fire fighting in Cardiff. As a result of local government reorganisation the former Cardiff City Fire Service in 1973 became part of the new County of South Glamorgan Fire Service and the Adam Street building with only minor interior alterations became the County Fire Headquarters.

And All That Jazz . . .

by John Scantlebury

CARDIFF WAS CAST in the classic mould to be a musically swinging city. Like the cradle of jazz, New Orleans, it had a quarter where the creeds and cultures of a multitude of races mixed pulsatingly to provide virtually the sole entertainment.

Dockland has been the spiritual home of Cardiff jazz musicians down the years, even when a surge of interest north of Bute Terrace would lure them to the city centre pubs or clubs. Yet there was always a special appeal in playing a Docks carnival or club. Sadly, redevelopment has savagely reduced such opportunities but that old feeling lingers and there's nostalgia aplenty for the old nights at the Ghana club or the *Quebec* hotel.

But to begin at the beginning . . . Well, that's just about impossible because how do you define where rhythm music stops and jazz begins?

But if there was a father of jazz in Cardiff it was accordionist Tony Chadgidakis and if there was a birthplace it was the *Great Windsor* hotel near Pier Head in the late 'thirties. One of the city's legendary musicians, Vic Parker, was in at the beginning.

For Vic jazz was an escape from playing in the Latin American bands that were booming then. 'We'd go on till midnight and then I'd go down to the dives, the cellars, and sit in with the jazz musicians.

'Tony was king. All the jazz fellows in London, he would walk in and kill them all. Even Shearing. He used to play accordion but when he heard Tony . . .

'There'd be Sunday sessions, Shearing on piano, Tony and another Docks boy, Joe Deniz, on guitar. I remember Tommy Whittle, Johnny Dankworth, just kids, coming in and asking for a sit-in'.

Vic and Tony would return to Cardiff frequently and they brought the new music with them.

It was something of a shock for the city. Jazz records were unknown and the music of Dockland was of its inhabitants—African, West Indian, Portuguese. Tony and Vic set about spreading the message.

'Ray Noman picked it up from us and we used to meet in the Windsor on a Saturday night, lock ourselves in the smoke room and play', recalls Vic. 'Nobody wanted to listen. There'd be Tony, myself, Ray, Billy Driscoll and Albert Lovell—nearly all guitar players, you notice. There weren't any horns around then.

'Drums? No, there weren't any drummers until

much later on. Basil Murphy was the first, I think.

'Ray could have been a great guitarist—he taught me a lot later on. But he had a sort of inferiority complex. If only he could have pushed himself.

'Maurice Grant was another great musician. He played organ and piano, wonderful at jazz, or any other sort of music for that matter. He could play the lot'.

Cardiff just before the war was not quite ready for jazz. 'We tried to get it going up town, we tried hard, but we couldn't. They didn't want to know—they just wanted the old tunes. Yes, trying to play jazz in the 'thirties was disheartening'.

But within a few years things were changing.

the name bands were playing at the Capitol and the New Theatre and the great exiled French violinist, Stephane Grappelly came down with Joe Deniz and his brother Frank who were making their name nationally.

'Joe was tremendous', says Vic Parker. 'One note from him and the whole thing was away. He was a marvellous Hawaiian steel guitar player too—you should have heard him playing jazz on that'.

The third Deniz brother, Laurie, was also a fine guitar player, although he tended to play more Cuban rhythm music than jazz.

Besides staging the big bands the Capitol had its own sextet which incorporated a fair amount

The legendary Vic Parker holds court in the now-defunct *Quebec*. 'It was the greatest', he says
Photograph courtesy Western Mail and Echo Ltd

66

The Phillips-Hawkes All Stars
featuring Terry Hawkes (drums),
Mabon Abrahams (piano), N.
Mills (bass), Jeff Phillips (trumpet), Pete Curtis (clarinet), and
Ian Forsythe (trombone)

of jazz in its repertoire. The group, which won the *Melody Maker* Dance Band Championship in 1942 certainly had the right instrumentation, with Jack Evans (alto), Tommy Marriott (clarinet), Garfield Ireland (trumpet), Billy Christelow (piano), Ossie Meredith and Joe Thomas (drums).

Then there was Cardiff Rhythm Club, holding twice-weekly meetings at St Dyfrig's Hall in Riverside. Mainstays were Terry Dyke (an early exponent of the electric guitar), Billy Rowlands (another fine guitarist) and Dennis O'Shea on drums and they would be joined by sitters-in, including some 'names' on leave from the Forces.

Cardiff jazzologist Skeets Hurford recalls a Cyncoed Rhythm Club and drummer Alan Carslake's Woodchoppers, who played around 1940. Goodman Quartet-influenced, the band's book nevertheless reflected the public's conservative tastes by including such swingy little numbers as 'Dearly Beloved', 'My Devotion' and 'I Remember You'.

There was no such compromise by the Geoff 'Elmer' Bright band, almost certainly Cardiff's first jazz band in the classic form. Bix Beiderbecke-Muggsy Spanier inspired, it had Bright on cornet, Ian Forsyth (trombone), Geoff Phillips

(drums), Alec Barbrooke (clarinet) and Doc Harris (piano). The Bright band played in church halls and other unlikely venues, generally outnumbering the listeners, and although short-lived it was an important spawning ground, as we shall see.

So the city's feet were beginning to tap, albeit reluctantly, when Vic Parker came back to the city for good in 1947. Ray Noman was soon around and the two set up sessions in the *Quebec* and the *Custom House* hotels.

'The *Quebec*—that turned out to be the greatest in the end, the place that brought jazz up to where it is now', says Vic.

'Mind you, at that time it was still just guitars. It was the guitar players who were most enthusiastic for jazz after hearing Django.

'It was only when we got to the *Quebec* that we had an audience, all the students. Don't ask me how they knew about jazz—maybe they didn't'!

The *Quebec* scene was to reach incredible proportions, especially when the Icon Jazzmen were resident in the sixties.

A national jazz magazine wrote lyrically about an old lady sitting outside in her rocking chair,

One of the clutch of youthful bands that sprang up around the late '50s—the Black River Jazz Band. Pictured are Brian Judd (clarinet), Hop Hurley (drums), Alun Rees (trumpet), Roy Shunter (guitar), Dai Greensmith (piano) and Rod Care (trombone)
Photograph by Bob Boothby

swaying to the music that poured from the windows. The writer's imagination was clearly working overtime but the *Quebec* did cast that sort of spell.

There was a great sense of loss among the musical fraternity when it closed down last year, although shadows of those great days can still be caught at the *Custom House* where Vic Parker now plays.

But I have raced ahead—we must return to the forties when jazz in Cardiff was still a wobbly babe . . .

As Vic Parker said, until this time jazz records were virtually unobtainable in the city but now they started to appear in Kinshott's, a record shop opposite the Castle. Armed with this new knowledge young enthusiasts—schoolboys and college students—began to make music.

The first major move came from Geoff Phillips, who had featured on drums in the Geoff Bright band. He now moved to trumpet and formed his own group which included a classical music recruit, Pete Curtis, on clarinet, Ian Forsyth (trombone), Tom Rosser (drums), Mabon Abrahams (piano) and Norman Mills (bass).

In 1951 Terry Hawkes came in on drums and the band became the fondly-remembered Phillips-Hawkes All Stars, a ubiquitous outfit that flitted about Cardiff until folding around 1956. The

band's venues included colleges, the CIAC's club at the top of Bute Street, the *Philharmonic* sessions (more about that later) and the Bowchier Hall—a real mixture. Forsyth and Hawkes were both to become members of the Acker Bilk band in Bristol for a short time.

All through its career the Phillips band and then the All Stars were vying for public acclaim with the bands of Mike Harries who had formed his first trio as a schoolboy clarinettist in 1944.

Harries was to become one of the three or four major influences on Cardiff's jazz scene, employing well over 100 musicians in his, so far, 33-year playing career.

A cousin of Geoff Bright, he began with front-room sessions with Martyn Hoskins on trumpet and Eric Weekly on banjo.

Bix and Condon were the only influences available to them and the three boys didn't really know what they were doing. 'We used to spend weeks learning The Saints', Harries recalls.

Then in 1946 the release of the Bunk Johnson records pushed him in a completely new direction and Cardiff's first attempted New Orleans jazz band saw him with Clive Thomas (trombone), T. I. N. Thomas (trumpet), Gethin John (three-string banjo), Graham Smithson (drums) and Ron Williams (piano).

The band made its debut at the Sybil Marks-

68

Phil Williams School of Dancing Saturday night hop where boogie-woogie and jive were on the curriculum.

By the beginning of the 'fifties Harries had switched to trombone to make room for clarinettist Brian Leake (now playing piano for the Alan Elsdon band) and the scene was set for the launching of Cardiff's really successful jazz club at the *Philharmonic* hotel in St Mary Street.

Leake went off to National Service like so many budding jazzmen at this time and Acker Bilk was hired for several jobs for £2. 14s. 6d., out of which he had to pay his travel expenses.

The *Philharmonic* scene lasted until 1956 and in later years there came the clubs at 7 High Street (where Saturday night queues would stretch around St John's Church), the Estonian Club (which saw visits from such New Orleans legends as George Lewis, Kid Thomas Valentine, Emanuel Paul and Alton Purnell), the Dockland Stork Club (where Harold Dejan visited) and the *Tredegar Arms* pub in Bute Terrace.

Other stars brought to Cardiff by the Harries bands were altoist Capt. John Handy and trumpeter Kid Sheik who featured in a concert at the Reardon Smith Lecture Theatre. Jazz was growing socially acceptable!

It would be impossible to list all the Harries line-ups but these are just some of his sidesmen over the years. Trumpets: John Hummerstone, Brian Savigar, Brian Benger, John Everett and John Bridges.

Reeds: Andy Warren, Charlie Blackburn, Pete Lenahan, Jim Criddle, Pete Chapman, Tony Dockrell and myself.

Bass: Ed Fox, John Silva, Kevin O'Sullivan, Ed. Bird, 'Teddy' Bear, John Couch and Mike Stamp.

Piano: Howell Bines, Brian Ford and Eric Herbert.

One of the many Mike Harries line-ups, this one *c*.1962. John Scantlebury is on clarinet, John Hummerstone (trumpet), Eddie Williams (banjo), and Mike Harries (trombone)
Photograph courtesy Western Mail and Echo Ltd

Drums: Tom Rosser, John Bennett and Clarence Nugent.

Banjo: Eddie Williams, Meic Stephens, Roy Davies and Lynn Saunders.

The current Mike Harries Band plays at Chapter Arts Centre on Fridays.

The lengthy career of Mike Harries has taken us forward a long way. We must now go back to the early 'fifties when the jazz scene was expanding rapidly.

In 1951 a youthful dance band which had Kenyon Owen on banjo and guitar, John Hummerstone on trumpet, Cyril Keefer on clarinet and John Bennett on drums found themselves drifting towards jazz.

After a year's pause while Owen and Bennett played with the Harries band, they reunited, now as the Riverside Jazz Band, swapping Hummerstone with Harries trumpet man Brian Savigar.

Owen was now playing trombone and the band gigged at the *Philharmonic* and the Estonian Club in Charles Street, using a Chicago-Dixie format.

The Riverside operated until around 1955 and on its break-up Bennett was another Cardiff musician who found a job in the Bilk band.

In 1959, out of National Service, he met trumpeter Keith Jenkins and the Castle City Jazz Band was born. Playing at the Castle Ballroom opposite Cardiff Castle it had Pete Locke (trombone), Nigel Carney and later Ceri Davies (clarinet), Brian Keene or Mike Hobbs (banjo) and Robin Beynon (drums). Eventually the band moved its base to Newport, the home of most of its members. Bennett, incidentally, had one more Cardiff fling when he operated the nationally-owned but ill-fated Chinese Jazz Club and the Victoria Ballroom in the early 'sixties.

A New Orleans welcome to Cardiff for two N.O. greats, Kid Thomas Valentine and Emanuel Paul, from the Adamant Brass Band, made up of musicians from several jazz outfits in the city. The Adamant are still going strong raising money for charity

Photograph courtesy Western Mail and Echo Ltd

Bill Burgwyn, a much-admired trombonist, in an outdoor set at Glantaff School in 1965 with trumpeter Bev Luen and clarinettist Alun Jones, now reed man with the Icon Jazzmen

Of the deceased Riverside band Brian Savigar was to play on for a little while, leading the Blue Blood Jazzmen who had perhaps had the strangest niche of any of Cardiff's jazz outfits.

Home for them was the caves in quarry workings near the Garth Mountain in which they set up the Prehistoric Club. It was a venture that was not to last long, although it would be interesting to see how such a club would succeed now when most fans have ready transport and an urge to hear their music in 'different' surroundings.

While the trad. bands were thriving there had been important developments on the small group scene. A London pro drummer, Parry England, a Barry boy, had come down to Cardiff some years before and become manager of the Continental Restaurant in Queen Street. He introduced there the first-ever star jazz sessions in the city and in the mid-fifties took on a trio led by drummer Mike Pincombe. It was the start of a long association with jazz for the Continental: Pincombe, with Ken Harding (piano) and Peter Morgan (bass) played their Shearing-Garner type music there for a decade before handing on to the Austin Davies Trio who did a slightly longer stint—almost certainly the longest residency of anyone in Cardiff.

Davies, who had had a jazz quartet in a radio series and ran a group called the Delta 5, still has an excellent group today, with bass guitarist Terry

Greenslade and drummer John Stark. Among the people they have backed are Don Rendell, Danny Moss, Tommy Whittle, Pete King, Bill Le Sage, Bobby Lamb and Duncan Lamont.

Also in this school came Dave Gill who was to leave Cardiff to play his music on the Atlantic luxury liners. We shall hear more about him later.

By the end of the 'fifties the trad. boom was chug-chugging away merrily and more and more young musicians were appearing. Llanishen Youth Club, for example, produced the Black River Jazz Band, led by Alun Rees, a forceful trumpet player, and with an excellent clarinettist and alto player, Brian Judd. Completing the line-up were Rodney Care (trombone), David Greensmith (piano), Roy Shunter (guitar) and John Hurley (drums).

Then there was the Apex Jazzmen who met at the *Pineapple* pub in Llandaff North for over two years. This again featured David Greensmith, by now experimenting with double bass, Alun Jones, now reed man with the Icon Jazzmen, and Bill Burgwyn, a fine relaxed trombonist. Mike Roberts, 'Bug' Craven and later Bev. Luen (trumpet), John Evans (banjo) and Colin Jones (drums) completed the outfit.

In 1963 a London trombonist came on the scene who was to be another mighty influence on Cardiff

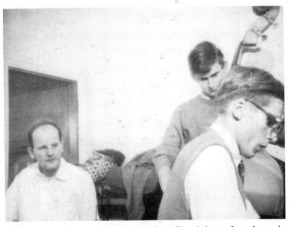

Scientist and broadcaster Brian Ford is a fine boogie piano player and was prominent on the Cardiff scene in the late '50s and early '60s. Here he's in action at Newbridge Arts Ball with drummer Tom Rosser and bassist Kevin O'Sullivan in 1960

The polished Austin Davies Trio played a long stint at the New Continental's Victoriana Suite. Apart from Austin Davies on piano the trio consists of Terry Greenslade on bass and John Stark on drums
Photograph by Haydn Baynham

music. The Tim Wacher Jump Band was the first mainstream group in the city, featuring trumpet, clarinet, two saxes, trombone and rhythm. Incidentally, it played some of the first arrangements by the developing Dave Greensmith.

In autumn 1964 the band started regular sessions at the Middle Eight Jazz Club at the British Legion Club in Womanby Street, the band's home for a year in which the high spot was a concert featuring bluesman Champion Jack Dupree.

Personnel at various times was Alan Jones or Jeff Meredith (trumpet), Brian Judd or Tony Roberts (alto/clarinet), Tim Wacher (trombone),

Eric Herbert (piano), Geoff Cook, John Silva or Dave Greensmith (bass), Rob Harris or Alex Humphreys (drums) and occasionally Mel Nunley, a tenor player from Pontypool, last heard of teaching woodwork in Zambia!

The band broke up when Wacher returned to London around 1966 but it had opened up a new avenue for music in Cardiff, soon to be taken by the Welsh Jazz Orchestra, later known as the Eric Wetherell Big Band.

The orchestra was originally led by John Williams, a baritone saxophonist and another Londoner. At that time he was playing in the dance band at the Top Rank Suite and, in a 30-years-on parallel with Vic Parker, formed a spare-time jazz outfit as an opportunity for the frustrated Rank musicians to play more interesting music.

The band used to perform at the Tower Club in Penarth Road but moved eventually to the New Moon Club where for several years concerts were held approximately monthly, usually featuring nationally-known guest musicians.

In 1968 Eric Wetherell, assistant MD with the Welsh National Opera, took over musical direction and concentrated on bringing the band up to a very high standard which it retains to this day.

The band has made many TV and radio broadcasts and appeared at nearly all the local music and arts festivals, but its very size (25 approx.) means it is expensive and with a growing introvertness it is now making fewer public appearances.

Nevertheless it rehearses from September to April at Churchills in Cardiff Road, Llandaff, on Sunday lunchtimes, developing a very contemporary style and playing a lot of jazz-rock numbers.

Out of the WJO came the New Welsh Jazz Sextet, again led by John Williams, with a complement that included Nick Evans who later moved to London and played with the Brotherhood of Breath, Keith Tippett, Graham Collier, etc.

Ian Forsyth, whom we met in the early stages of this story, now surprisingly reappears in the modern Karl Jenkins-Roger Parker Quintet which was formed in 1965. According to David Greensmith, this band probably reached the highest standard of modern jazz ever heard in Cardiff and Karl Jenkins went on to play with such luminaries as Graham Collier, Ian Carr's Nucleus and Soft Machine.

An early modern avant garde group was the Tony Faulkner Sextet which played from 1968 to 1970. A drummer from the North of England, Faulkner led the band in a residency at Tiffany's in St Mary Street. He later won a scholarship to the Berklees School of Music in Boston, U.S.A.

Drummer Mike Pincombe ran a highly accomplished trio for many years. The bass player, Peter Morgan, now works with the Dudley Moore Trio and with Roy Budd, among others

Swingtime at the New Moon club—the new Welsh Jazz Orchestra in rehearsals in 1966
Photograph courtesy Western Mail and Echo Ltd

but for some reason didn't take it up.

The line-up of the sextet was Faulkner, Kenvin Evans (trumpet), Sean O'Brien (tenor), Daryl Williams (trombone), Roger Parker (piano), later replaced by Paul Matthews who is currently musical director for top singer Buddy Greco.

Back on the traditional scene the Icon Jazzmen were brought together in 1969, principally by Roy Davies who had played banjo with the Saratoga Jazz Band at the *Albert* hotel in St Mary Street. These had also featured trombonist Geoff Palser, trumpeter Bill Kemp, drummer Mike Pearce, clarinettist Alun Jones and, once again, David Greensmith. Gary Plank (bass) and Tony Denton (drums) were also sometime members.

Davies enlisted trumpeter John Bridges, drummer Clarence Nugent and myself, on alto, from a recently-split Mike Harries band and also drew former Harries pianist Howell Bines back to the keyboard.

It was this band, unrelentingly hot after the jazz-dance investigations of the erstwhile Harries band, that moved into the *Quebec*. With Vic Parker, and sometimes Ray Noman playing the interval, good music came as thickly as the nicotine on the old pub's walls.

Eddie Williams, another former Harries sidesman, took over from Roy Davies, never an enthusiastic public performer and Alun Jones took over on alto and clarinet when I retired. Bob

Tunnicliffe filled the vacant trombone square foot (there was never room for a chair) but when Geoff Palser returned from a few years in London he took over, with Tunnicliffe switching to bass. The upheavals continued with John Bridges's retirement.

While Bill Kemp took the trumpet chair briefly Gloucester horn-man John Keene helped out for several months. But waiting in the wings was a 16-year-old who was to become perhaps the biggest influence of all on the Cardiff jazz scene—Chris Hodgkins.

Hodgkins recalls: 'The guy who really struck me was John Bridges—when I first heard live jazz at the age of 15 J.B. was the guy. Although my brother played trumpet John was my man—

he had all that fire'. (It is almost certain that only illness stopped the enigmatic Bridges becoming one of the best New Orleans-Chicago trumpet players in Britain. He is now happily coming back on the scene at the *Inn On The River*).

Despite his youth Hodgkins quickly brought some much-needed organisation into the traditional scene, and in 1973 it was he who brought the music back to the city centre when he took the Climax Band, a mainstream variation on the Icon band, to the *Great Western* hotel from the *Quebec*. The Icons as a whole soon followed and the *Western* scene of Sunday, Tuesday and Thursday full-house jazz was set. Continental tours, too, were soon part of the band's life.

The Icon line-up remained steady for two years

The Icon Jazzmen 'in session' at the *Quebec* hotel

until in October 1975 Hodgkins resigned to take a different musical path. The current Icons are Geoff Palser (trombone), Alun Jones (alto/clarinet), Paul Keele or Mike Palser (trumpet), Eddie Williams (banjo), Keith Little (piano) and Clarence Nugent (drums).

The first Chris Hodgkins Band had appeared at the *Bristol* hotel in Penarth Road in 1973 with Stuart Nicholson on tenor, Bob Tunnicliffe (trombone), Eric Herbert (piano), David Greensmith (bass) and Mike Pearce (drums).

On leaving the Icons Hodgkins put together a small group that included Eric Herbert, Bob Tunnicliffe and Lionel Davies but really took off with a new full band for the 1976 Welsh Jazz Festival.

The Hodgkins Band now dominates the South Wales jazz scene and was resident on HTV's Forum series early in 1977. Using London alto star Eric Gilchrist frequently, it has a highly polished and accomplished style.

The band is now at the *Royal* hotel on Sundays and at Chapter, the arts centre which is the new home for Chris Hodgkins's greatest contribution to Cardiff music, the Welsh Jazz Festival.

The idea for this arose, in fact, from a slightly-jokey conversation between Geoff Palser and Hodgkins and a pilot festival was launched in 1974. It has now grown into the largest such venture in Britain and the quality of visiting artists is growing each year.

At the same time Chris Hodgkins's career has

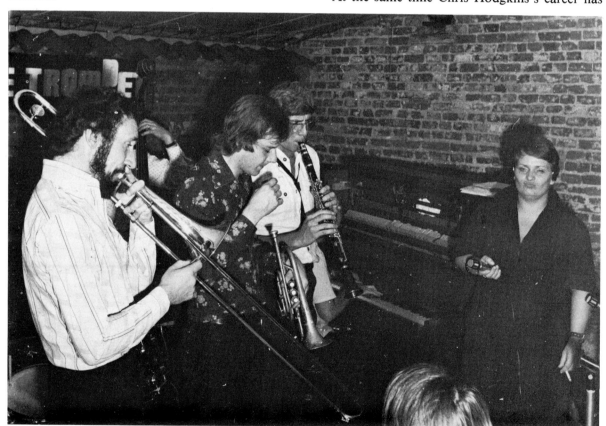

Spreading the Welsh sound—trumpeter Chris Hodgkins and his band in the Netherlands in 1976. Trombonist Bob Tunnicliffe runs his own group in Cardiff and the clarinettist is a regular guest with the Hodgkins band, London star Eric Gilchrist, obscuring pianist Eric Herbert

Part of the Tim Wacher band in rehearsal for a History of Jazz Concert at the Reardon-Smith Lecture Theatre in 1965. From left to right are Jeff Meredith, Tony Roberts, Tim Wacher, Mel Nunley and Dai Greensmith

also flourished. Now a full-time jazz musician, he has toured the Continent, notably with Monty Sunshine, and has travelled extensively with Dick Charlesworth, Johnny Bastable and Malc. Murphy.

But the highlights of his still young career must be the star guest nights with his own band at Chapter, which have seen Wild Bill Davison, Buddy Tate, Howard McGhee and Dick Carey in action.

Yet Chris is still a young man on the Cardiff jazz scene. One wonders what he can produce in the years to come if he manages to rebuff London's attractions.

Also in the mainstream track are the equally-proficient Bob Tunnicliffe Quintet, whose book is heavily accented to standards. The band features the outstanding bass of Lionel Davies and is completed by Mike Ludlow (tenor), Greg Evans (drums) and Colin Woodman (piano).

The most modern group around are Eclipse, formed in 1975. They have a present line-up of Neil Metcalfe (flute), Bob Jones (piano), John Schneider (electric guitar), Mark Griffiths (bass) and William Evans (drums).

Most of these bands now appear at Chapter,

one of the twin homes of Cardiff jazz in 1977, the other being the acclaimed *Inn On The River*. While Friday is 'open night', giving many musicians the chance to come out of virtual retirement for a blow, the staple diet for the *Inn* crowd is supplied on Tuesday evenings and Sunday lunchtimes by John Silva and his quintet.

For many people John Silva encapsulates the jazz story in Cardiff. A Docks lad, he was a jazz enthusiast who took up playing at a fairly late age (28) and went on to play in just about every style with some of the greatest musicians in the country.

It was in 1956 when he took up bass and joined the Geoff Phillips band but meeting Dave Gill set up a sideline band which played at the Students' Union in Dumfries Place on Saturday afternoons. Members were Viv Edwards (drums), Norman Beynon and Clive Hicks (guitar) and when the band moved to the CIAC's club in Bute Street Alf Williams joined on alto.

'We used to play again on Sunday afternoons and a lot of guys would drift in for a sit-in', says John. 'There'd be people like Benny James on trumpet, Rex Moon on trombone, who played with Langdon Doidge, and Bert Folland, a Ben

A thoughtful John Silva playing vibraphone at the *Inn on the River*. Also in the picture is Rob Haddon, guitar

Webster-style tenor player. A lot of the blokes were dance band guys who wanted a chance to play something more rewarding.

'It was a real jam session and we were probably the first guys to do any modern jazz—it was Clifford Brown sort of stuff, you know. This would be about 1962'.

Sessions followed at the Tower Club, with Ian McLellan on piano, Laurie Huxford (drums), Don Brooks, Bill Shaw or Bert Folland on tenor, plus guitarist Ray Noman.

'Then Gill and I formed another group with Roger Cummerford on drums, Alf Williams and Greg Bowen on trumpet. We'd go down to the Ghana Club, which my mother-in-law ran, on Saturday afternoons', recalls John. 'They had a juke box so we'd push the piano out the back and play there.

'All this time we were playing at the *Quebec*, the Tower Club and the BBC club. John Tyler was with me on drums for that one. I was also playing down Port Talbot and Swansea with Russ Jones, so it was a bit hectic'.

About 1963 John moved to the Ghana Club in earnest for Tuesday and Sunday sessions and started the famous star guest sets.

'For me that was the most successful club of them all', says John. 'The guys in London still talk about it. Nobody would come when we first planned it—they'd say "Cardiff? Ugghh".'

'Then I persuaded Tommy Whittle to come along and he enjoyed himself so much he started passing the word around. Then they all came —Don Rendell, Ian Carr, Danny Moss, Tubby Hayes, Duncan Lamont, Ronnie Ross . . . We had the Stan Tracey Quartet; they talk now about his Under Milk Wood Suite but the first time he played that was down the Ghana.

'Dave Goldberg came down three times and he wouldn't play jazz clubs in London.

'It got to the stage where I would invite a big guy down and they wouldn't even ask about the money. It was nice to be trusted like that. Of course a lot of guys we had down hadn't done anything much at that time although they've been big since. But in those days I was back and forth to London and I had a chance to hear them'.

The Ghana band had either John, Reg Chick or Lionel Davies on bass, Ian McLellan, Bernie Thorpe or Roy Pike on piano, Laurie Huxford or John Tyler on drums. When the club tumbled to the redevelopers the Silva outfit moved to the Stork Club, which saw visits from Harold McNair, Ian Carr, John McLaughlin and Danny Moss, and then the Ringside, which again had McNair as a guest as well as altoist Pete King.

'I was still busy because I was doing a gig at the Charleston Club with Cliff Anderson on piano and Benny Goodman on drums and also playing the Top Drawer Club, and that's when I started to play flute a bit. Then I dropped out of the Cardiff scene for a while when I worked in the Port Talbot-Swansea area'.

On his return John played the Stork Club and then when Chapter opened formed the first regular group there with Bob Jones, Lionel Davies, Dave Stephens and Alf Williams. McNair, King and Rendell were among the guests during the two-year stint.

The Chapter sessions finished in 1973 and John

A John Silva group playing at Chapter Arts Centre (left to right) Greg Evans (drums), Alf Williams (tenor sax), Lionel Davis (bass), John Silva (flute), obscuring Wallace Bloxham (piano)

A lively session at the Ghana Club with visiting star Dick Morrissey on tenor sax, backed by Ray Noman, guitar, and Lionel Davis, bass, among others

returned to the *Quebec* for sets with Vic Parker, Chris Hodgkins, Eric Herbert, Jed Williams and Bob Tunnicliffe, but a move to the *Sea Lock* saw him switching to vibes.

'I didn't start playing bass till I was 28, started flute at 38 and went on to vibes at 48. Maybe I'll think about guitar when I'm 58', says John.

The excellent Rob Haddon was then on guitar with Vince Rowles on drums and Phil Jones on bass and it was this band that moved to the *Inn On the River*. John Wakelin later joined on keyboards and when Phil Jones left Rob Haddon's father, Bill, moved in on bass.

Already the *Inn* has had special sessions with tenorist Barbara Thompson, vibes star Bill Le Sage and altoist Pete King.

John Silva has been instrumental in both giving Cardiff the best jazz in Britain and nurturing young talent, like Dave Barry and Dave Tidball, along the way; he has had the most intensive jazz

career of any in the city and his enthusiasm remains undiluted.

'That's all I did, man—play jazz. I didn't want to play nothing else'.

In the short space available here it hasn't been possible to detail all the individuals and characters who created the Cardiff jazz story—many, indeed, are recalled only hazily by some nickname or first name; Cardiff has turned out a legion of jazz makers who have taken the Welsh sound to many shores.

Now we see fathers and sons in several Cardiff bands as a new generation picks up its horns and prepares to blow the next chapter in the city's musical history.

As Victor Parker says: 'Thirty-odd years it's taken to get up to the standard it is now. I'd be happy if I never played again just to sit and listen to the boys today. It's wonderful to see so many people making such good music after all the spadework we put in . . .'

'Happiness is a Cigar . . .'

by Clive Pritchard

CARDIFF, ONE MIGHT THINK, has little in common with the ancient Mayan civilisations of Central America. Yet had those Mayan Indians not discovered the pleasures to be derived from puffing away at a roll of leaves from a local weed, the Capital City of Wales would have been deprived of one of its most modern industries.

Tobacco smoking formed part of the religious rites of the Mayan civilisations and today, two thousand or more years later, the factory of J. R. Freeman and Son Ltd. in Penarth Road, Cardiff, and its sister factory at Port Talbot, are at the heart of Britain's biggest cigar making operation.

Every year many millions of cigars are made on the sophisticated machines in these factories assisted by the skilled and nimble fingers of hundreds of Welsh girls, many of whom travel to Cardiff daily from the valleys.

If just one week's production of cigars from the Penarth Road factory were laid end to end they would stretch from Cardiff to London—a long haul from the days in 1839 when John Rykes Freeman finally decided there must be a market for a British made 'segar'.

The Duke of Wellington's men, in the true try-anything tradition of the British tommy, had acquired the cigar habit from Spanish guerrilla fighters. When the Duke's men came marching home and the cigar began catching on in Britain, Freeman went into production—and his first 'segar', fat in the middle and tapered at the ends, cost the early Victorian smoker a fraction of a penny.

Like most great men John Freeman was ahead of his time. Britain's market was historically a slow developer in terms of cigar smoking. Early in this century when Thomas Marshall was remarking about the USA that 'What this country needs is a good five-cent cigar' (and Will Rogers replying that 'We got plenty of good five-cent cigars. The trouble is that they cost fifteen'), the British (despite Freeman's five-a-penny product) still associated cigars with top hats and Rolls Royces—something you had to be very posh to enjoy. Few ordinary people would contemplate smoking a cigar, except perhaps to celebrate some special occasion when a cigar would be produced as a symbol of reckless extravagance. Even today, when cigar smoking has become a widespread habit, far more cigars are consumed around Christmas time than during the rest of the year.

Nevertheless the Freeman operation prospered to such an extent that in 1908 the firm moved from Shoreditch in London to Cardiff—a wise move if ever there was one! The first Cardiff location was in Bridge Street but later the factory moved to Grangetown where the first Manikin, destined to become Britain's biggest selling small cigar, was rolled in 1912.

In 1947 J. R. Freeman joined the Gallaher Group of Companies and developments and expansion proceeded apace. Production was moved into the temperature-controlled, scrupulously clean and carefully humidified Penarth Road factory in 1961.

It wasn't until the 'sixties that the old prejudices (to the effect that cigars were exclusively for the rich) began to break down. One of the reasons for this was the nation's growing affluence. People began to feel better off and, as a result, felt it less strange and ostentatious to smoke cigars. Since then, with the exception of one or two years of austerity, the cigar market has consistently grown.

Freeman were quick to respond to the challenge. They searched South Wales for a suitable site for a new factory and settled on Port Talbot. Here, after the successful establishment of a small,

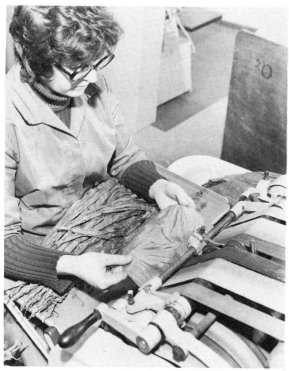

Nimble fingers manipulate the delicate cigar leaf

combined with Freeman's long-standing factory presence in Cardiff, placed South Wales in a dominant position in the cigar industry and gave the area an important position in the nation's vast tobacco trade.

A number of popular cigars are made at the Welsh factories but there can be no doubt that the two best known brands are Manikin and Hamlet which, between them, have dominated the small cigar market (known in the trade as large whiffs) for years. Both brands are famed for their television advertising—Manikin being associated with a series of very pretty girls and Hamlet with humorous advertisements on the theme 'Happiness is a cigar called Hamlet'.

It is perhaps of interest that Manikin, the long-time pace-maker, took its name from a pre-First World War music hall bill advertising an act called 'Little Mannikins'.

The cigar story starts a long way from the South Wales factories. The tobacco leaf is purchased from countries in many parts of the world, as far apart as the East and West Indies. By the careful blending of these tobaccos Freeman are able to cater for all smoking tastes—from the mild to the fuller flavoured cigars. Leaf experts from Cardiff visit the tobacco fields while the leaf is growing and take special care to purchase in the various world markets the right leaf for the

pilot plant, they built a large new factory at Baglan Moors and soon afterwards the head-quarters and administration of the Company moved from London to Cardiff. These moves,

The Cardiff factory of J. R. Freeman & Son Ltd

82

Counting and checking the finished cigars

grading and sizing of the leaves.

Irrespective of shape, size or colour all cigars contain three component parts—the filler, binder and wrapper, the last named being the finest possible leaf.

Handrolling days are gone—as sadly are the visions of dusky Cuban maidens with which that particular operation was associated—but Freeman still use many of the traditional processes, speeded up with the aid of machines. And when the cigars have been made but before they are packed, the moisture introduced into the leaf to make it pliable must be removed and this is done in an atmosphere which simulates the natural conditions in which cigars have traditionally been brought to the ideal moisture content to give a perfect smoke.

Throughout the factory emphasis is laid on the need for smooth, uninterrupted flow of materials and products with the minimum amount of human handling. The aim is to achieve all the best qualities of the old hand-made cigar at an economical price. One of the things that makes this possible is the design of the factory (be it Cardiff or Port Talbot) which is all on one floor and allows for large open and unobstructed working areas.

Expansion and improvement is a constant process at the Freeman factories which claim to be the most modern of their kind in Europe. The latest programme, recently completed at a cost of £1.5 million, doubled the production area at the Port Talbot factory—an area now large enough to accommodate a couple of football pitches. And a new cigar store there can accommodate up to 120 million cigars—a figure which gives a clue to the size and importance of the Freeman operation in South Wales.

different brands.

When the raw leaf arrives at the factory in bales or cases worth thousands of pounds each, it is dry and brittle and has firstly to be preconditioned by introducing sufficient moisture to render it workable. Throughout manufacture great care is taken to see that the leaf is not damaged and the factory atmosphere is kept at a constant humidity and temperature to ensure that it remains pliable.

The removal of the stem, an essential feature of cigar manufacture, is largely carried out manually by highly skilled and specially trained girls who are also responsible for the colour

Long-lost *Ely*sian Fields

by Roy Denning

WHEN THE ROMANS came to Ely they were by no means the first to seize upon that delectable spot. The local Silures, a wildly independent bunch of citizens much given to inter-tribal warfare and cattle-raiding, soon found that they could not match the imperial infantry, who were unsportingly clad in protective armour. So they took to the trackless hills and contented themselves with occasional forays, thus establishing a tradition still observed by their descendants on international days.

Half-hidden in the wooded slopes to the south of Ely rises the Caerau hill-fort, twelve acres of grassland surrounded by earthen embankments. A sombre place it is, steeped in uneasy mystery, a dark monument half-hinting at a way of life just glimpsed in the corner of the mind's eye. Certainly, in its heyday some two thousand years ago it must have dominated the landscape, its massive banks surmounted by a stout timber palisade and its curving eastern entrance, decorated with skulls of luckless enemies, closely guarded by keen-eyed sentinels. Whether the Romans, as was their custom with tribal strongholds, took the place by fire and sword nobody knows, for there has been no excavation to answer the question, neither do we know if it was inhabited when the first of the new style settlers built his villa on the site of the old Ely racecourse. Excavations by the late Sir Mortimer Wheeler in 1922 showed that a building, dated to the early second century AD, was constructed in an area which was then marshland. It was equipped with an efficient hypocaust heating system, unrivalled in Ely till the advent of microbore. But the sea raiders who swarmed up the Channel from the fourth to the ninth centuries took a poor view of such effeminate home comforts and the villa, either abandoned by its inhabitants or wrecked by the raiders, crumbled into ruin and the glutinous marsh reclaimed its own.

The Roman road through the Vale, linking west Wales and the venerable town of Caerwent, decided the location of Ely, for it crossed the river at the lowest fordable point above the sea, which was some five hundred yards north of the villa, at a place which was later known as 'Rhyd Sarn'. On the eastern bank the road forked, one branch following the rising ground to another ford at Llandaff, and the other, the present Cowbridge road, taking the lower and marshier route. No doubt a tiny settlement, consisting of a few wattle-and-daub huts and an inn, would have grown up at the ford during the twilight of the Roman occupation. If so, the infant Ely was to suffer a long, harsh childhood, for soon came the intermittent desperation of the dark ages, when Cardiff itself seems to have been abandoned and civilisation's brief candle sputtered fitfully.

Now from the west came the fiery Celtic saints, full of missionary zeal and other worldliness, eager to put a spiritual arm-lock on the demoted pagan gods and hustle them post-haste to Hell. Primitive churches appeared throughout the Vale, while at Dinas Powis, a few miles to the south, a fortified dark age settlement has yielded evidence that there was even a small amount of trade with the Continent.

The first evidence we have of the revival of organised life in the Ely area after the Danish raids is the ring-work which occupies the north-east corner of Caerau hill-fort. This, though apparently based on a Continental model, is probably a native Welsh construction. Its position, dominating the south-west part of the Cardiff basin, possibly indicates the stronghold of some emergent local chieftain, or perhaps a fortified homestead, while it seems to pre-date the Norman invasion. The Ely district was now part of the kingdom of Morgannwg, whose last prince, a person of dubious repute named Iestyn ap Gwrgant, was overthrown by Robert Fitzhamon and his band of freebooters in a battle on Mynydd Bychan (the Crwys Road area) in the year 1093. With the subsequent founding of Norman Cardiff came the organisation of the local manors upon feudal lines, the purpose of which was to support the knightly conquerors in their expensive life-style of hunting, carousing and fighting. The little riverside settlement now found itself incorporated in the manor of Llandaff and in the possession of the bishop, medieval bishops considering them-selves potentates of this world as well as strong candidates for preferment in the next.

The earliest literary reference to Ely as a settle-ment belongs to the bishopric of Urban, bishop of Llandaff from 1107 to 1133, when the hamlet of Ely was named as one of the chapelries of Llandaff. The middle ages saw the general rise of a tradition of bridge building, an activity which ranked as a work of piety, and to this period belongs the first-known Ely bridge, a stone struc-ture at a time when the bridges at Cardiff and Llandaff were built of wood. As was then customary, a small chapel stood nearby for the pious and charitable to perform their devotions, leaving an offering for the good of their souls and the upkeep of the bridge, the chapel and attendant priest.

At this time Ely lay on the pilgrim route to St David's, two trips to which were reckoned as being equal to a pilgrimage to Rome, such was the uncertainty of travel through medieval Wales. As late as the beginning of the 19th century a small plot of land alongside the A48, just west of the recently-demolished Saintwell chapel, was known as 'Sanctuary', being probably a resting place for pilgrims. There was here a holy well

THE GROWTH OF ELY

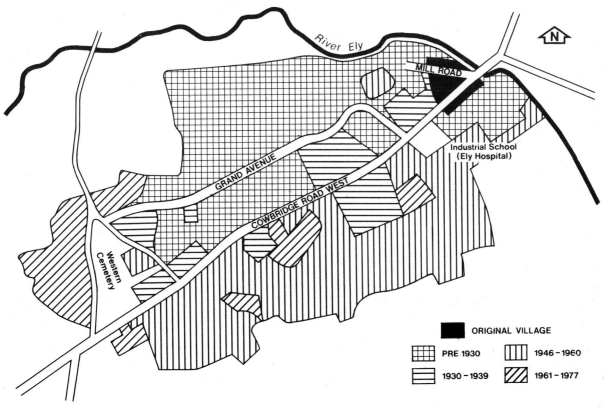

ORIGINAL VILLAGE

PRE-1930   1946-1960

1930-1939   1961-1977

which gave rise to the later alternative name of 'Saintwell'. Incidentally, there is no authority for calling this area 'Cyntwell', an artificial Anglo-Welsh hybrid, mistakenly taken to be the origin of the local pronunciation 'Sintwell'.

The modern A48, roaring ostentatiously through Ely with a promise of certain extinction for the unwary pedestrian, bears little resemblance except its course to the minor country road it has replaced, though its running costs have increased in direct proportion to the discomfort it inflicts on the unfortunate suburb. The old road, however, itself lacked nothing in discomfort, being little more than a muddy track. In 1590 it was reported to the Quarter Sessions that the 'highe waye ledynge from Cardyff bridge to Eley bridge' was 'insufficient'. It continued 'insufficient' till the building of the turnpike road in the 1760s, when it was widened and straightened. During widening operations near the *Dusty Forge* (then known as *Efail y Dwst*) some human bones were found, a possible relic of the Battle of St Fagans in 1648, or more likely a grim reminder that our ancestors could be as conveniently forgetful as any of their descendants in their observance of the law. Before the establishment of village shops the smaller requirements of the country folk were met by travelling pedlars, very often Scottish packmen. These men took their lives in their hands, for they were an easy target and frequently ended their days with a knife in the ribs, their bodies hastily buried in the nearest ditch. There are records of several such casual murders, particularly in the Wrinston area.

After the Reformation, Ely Bridge, having entered a pragmatic age when piety and charity had no longer the mind-bending force of former days, fell upon evil times and was often 'presented' to the Sessions as being 'out of repair', the cost of the repairs to be borne by the rate-payers of the parish. However dilapidated, it was still considered important enough one sunny morning in May 1648 for Colonel Horton, the Parliamentary commander, to station there a detachment of troopers with the object of denying the bridge to the Royalists, who were then advancing on Cardiff. The seizure of Ely may well have had a decisive effect on the course of the Civil War, for the out-manoeuvred Royalists chose to advance along an alternative route through St Fagans, where they were shattered in a conflict after which, according to legend, the Ely river ran red with blood.

Gradually the village grew, till by the reign of Charles II it consisted of thirty-four households and farms, as shown by the hearth tax assessments. Seventeen of these households were too poor to be taxed. Ely was now a substantial farming village, supporting small craftsmen who also farmed a few acres. This mixed economy continued to at least the middle of the 19th century, for the census returns of 1851 show that Mary Lewis, who kept the *Ely Bridge Inn*, also farmed eight acres, while Griffith David, miller, of Ely Mills, farmed twenty-five acres. Ely Mills stood beside the river at the end of Birdie's lane and the walls were still standing some twenty years ago. The high spot of the rural year in the 18th century was the annual fair which was held on 22 July. It was the occasion for innocent country pastimes, such as bull-baiting, cock-fighting, brawling with one's neighbours and being carried home in the early hours of the morning. Amusement was rough and home-made, but any self-respecting village could boast a fiddler of some talent. William Jenkin of Ely farm was such a man, though he was blind.

Rustic manners did not feel the restraining hand of Methodism until the second half of the 18th century, when John Wesley, travelling in reverse the paths of the dark age missionaries, was instrumental in putting down these entertainments. Some degree of restraint was apparently overdue, for drunkenness was very common. In July 1766 Philip Evan of Ely allegedly murdered his wife by beating her to death for selling the cheese and butter as soon as it was made in order to buy beer. The wife was perpetually drunk, while Philip was himself drunk at the time and may well have been incensed at his spouse getting her hands on the money before him. He was committed to Cardiff gaol and clapped in the heaviest irons, while his wife, a native of Colwinston, was returned to her home village for burial. Philip was eventually acquitted, asserting in his defence that his wife had fallen down the stairs, though he could not explain how the body was found upstairs, beside the bed.

With the dawn of the 19th century a new awareness of religion came to Ely. The nearest Anglican churches, Llandaff cathedral and St Mary's, Caerau, had made little impact on the area, but Welsh Methodism, fiercely disapproving of the rural sports beloved of the previous era, appealed to the latent puritanism of the rising middle class and a compulsive respectability gradually permeated society. In 1806 Thomas Morgan, owner of a smallholding in Mill Road, was moved to donate a barn and thirteen perches of land for use as a church yard. The converted barn did yeoman service till 1843, when it was renovated at a cost of approximately three hundred pounds. Owing chiefly to the energetic leadership of some of the ladies of the village, notably Mrs George Thomas of Ely farm and Mrs Elizabeth Thomas of Glyn Teg Hall (which later became, ironically, the offices of the Ely Brewery Company) a new chapel was built in 1857 on the site of the old barn.

If any one event can be said to have changed the structure of society in Ely that event must surely be the coming of the railway in 1850. The census returns for 1841 show a population of 215 consisting almost exclusively of labourers and rural craftsmen and their dependents. By 1851 the population had grown to 281 and now included many people from the west of England, such as the Bushnell family from Clovelly, the Baskervilles from Bratton and the Gibbs from Bath. By 1861 the population had risen to 360. The English people were mostly concerned with the railway, Thomas H. Gibbs being described in 1851 as 'Clerk to the Railway Company', a term of the utmost sophistication in rural Wales, while no less than seven Ely men found employment as railway labourers. The advent of the English folk im-

Mill Road corner about 1906

mediately began to change a community where the language had been exclusively Welsh, and by 1858 services in both English and Welsh were being conducted in the chapel. Whatever the stimulus to religion, it was the kiss of death for *yr hen iaith*. In 1879 the Wesleyan chapel was sold to the English Wesleyan Connexion and by about 1900 Welsh was heard no more in the village.

Until 1869 Ely was a hamlet within the ecclesiastical parish of Llandaff and the Anglican inhabitants attended Llandaff cathedral or St Mary's, Caerau, if that church were nearer. In addition, Thursday services were held by the Rev. C. B. Bevan, a canon of the cathedral, in the kitchen of a thatched cottage in Mill Road, a site subsequently occupied by Grover's Terrace (built in 1871). In 1869 Ely was transferred to the living of St Mary's and the new church of St David's, Cowbridge Road, was consecrated on 23 November 1871. One of the first churchwardens was George Thomas of Ely farm, whose wife was one of the chief supporters of the main nonconformist rivals, the Wesleyan Methodists. George Thomas, a native of Pentyrch and father of Sir Illtyd Thomas, was one of the last Welsh speakers in Ely.

The construction of the Barry railway in 1889 brought an influx of labourers into the Saintwell area. The souls of these workers, of a class not noted for sobriety or religious observance, became the concern of William Windsor, who was instrumental in erecting a temporary chapel, known as the 'Navvies Mission', at the junction of Cwrt-yr-Ala lane and Cowbridge Road. This was replaced by a red-brick building (Saintwell Congregational Church) in 1907, which was itself demolished a few years ago when the congregation moved to a new church in Heol Trelai. Later religious developments in Ely were the advent of Baptist, Roman Catholic and Presbyterian churches, while Grand Avenue United Reform Church (then Congregational) was opened in 1927 as a daughter church of Saintwell. The Church of the Resurrection, Grand Avenue, followed in 1934, replacing a large ex-Church Army hut, which had been brought from Lincolnshire ten

years previously. The site of the hut is now occupied by Glanely Hall. The Wesleyans, having outgrown the old church in Mill Road, built a new church which was opened in 1911 on a site at the corner of Cowbridge Road and Colin Way (then called Paget Road).

Development followed at a steady but decorous pace in the wake of the railway. The first resident police constable, one David Bowen, was appointed in the 1870s, while the Cardiff Union Industrial Schools (now the Ely Children's Homes) were built in Cowbridge Road in 1862 to provide suitable training for orphan children. At the turn of the century the Industrial Schools were converted into a workhouse for the aged and infirm, with five 'Cottage Homes' attached for the children. Light industry began to appear from the 'sixties on, Ely Paper Mills being commenced in 1865 by Messrs. Brown and Evans. The Tower Brewery was built near the railway station, Chivers pickle factory was moved from Grangetown to Ely in 1890 and Crosswell's brewery followed soon after. Cardiff Racecourse was laid out round the Volunteer Rifle Range behind the Industrial Schools.

At the turn of the century Ely still presented the picture of a village, set amid green countryside, farm and market gardens. The largest farm, of 300 acres, was Ty Coch, then becoming known as 'Red House' farm, while Ely farm, of 70 acres, lay to the south. Green farm, then in the parish of Michaelston-super-Ely, and Sweldon, the ancient home of the Mathew family in Caerau parish, were not yet threatened by urban sprawl. Fairwater, too, slumbered peacefully in rural seclusion. To the east the village was separated from Canton by Ely Common, part of which was to become Victoria Park in 1897. By 1920 Pencisely Road, Ely Road and Windway Road were beginning to assume their present character, substantial new houses replacing the old-style white-washed cottages. Mill Road was narrow, with a bottleneck near the entrance from Cowbridge Road which caused difficulties when the new bus service started. At the spot where

Herbert Thompson School now stands Mill Road petered out into an occupation road leading up the hill to Red House farm. From the farm two footpaths led to Cowbridge Road; one led beside a dingle and pond to emerge at the present junction of Grand Avenue and Cowbridge Road, while the other led to the place where Crossways Road now joins the main road. There was also a footpath through swing gates and across a market garden from a point opposite St David's church to Mill Road, coming out just north of the site of the Regent cinema.

Westwards from St David's to Culverhouse Cross the only houses on the north side of the road at this time were a row of four cottages (Britway Terrace or 'Bowen's Row') opposite the Isolation Hospital, an old one-storey turnpike cottage, 'Highmead', the home of the well-known Vachell family, 'Ash Cottage' and the *Dusty Forge*. On the south side there were but four dwelling-houses (three of them at the Caerau lane junction) between the Isolation Hospital and Saintwell.

After the finish of the First World War the booming city of Cardiff was poised to expand yet again. Roath, Grangetown and Canton had been absorbed in 1875 and in 1922 it was the turn of Llanishen, Llandaff and Ely to experience the inevitable. Compulsory purchase orders had been issued in February 1920 for Green farm and Red House farm, at sums respectively of £31,000 and £40,000. The present day values of such quantities of prime development land would probably give even the average oil-rich Arabian sheikh pause for thought.

The growth of Ely to its present size was a long process. First came the roads in the vicinity of Red House farm, such as Archer Road, Frank Road, Llewellyn Avenue, Pethybridge Road, the lower end of Grand Avenue and the commemorative Ty Coch Road. The houses in these areas, both terraced and semi-detached, were often roofed with red tiles, tending to create a warm and welcoming appearance, but the sombre, black timber houses at the junction of Phyllis Crescent and Mill Road (some destroyed by fire)

Laying of the foundation stones for the Ely Methodist Church, Cowbridge Road, November 1910

lent no charm to the scene. 'Dutch parlour-type' houses, unusually spacious for the time, were built here and there along Grand Avenue and Red House Crescent, and at various corner sites, in a laudable attempt to vary the monotony of council estate building, while each house had a reasonable garden, back and front. Red-brick flats with semi-circular pediments were also erected in Grand Avenue, which has in recent years been much improved by the thoughtful planting of trees. By 1930 the tide of building had rolled westward up the hill, reaching Mostyn Road, Snowden Road, MacDonald Road and Green Farm Road, with Marcross Road, Meyrick Road and Penmark Road being added in the immediate pre-war years, together with an infilling in the Vachell Road area. Hywel Dda school in Cambria Road was opened on St David's Day, 1934, to supplement the earlier 'Old Ely', Windsor Clive, Herbert Thompson and St Francis schools. In 1939 the advent of the War put an effective, if temporary, stop to further development.

Though it was apparent by 1938 that destruction was the probable theme of the next few years, the Corporation decided to proceed with the acquisition of Sweldon farm, a site of historic interest, from the Wharton estate. In February 1939 Sweldon farm was bought at auction for £12,400, the sale not including the house and eighteen acres. At that time virtually the only housing south of Cowbridge Road was a limited amount of private building near the Western Welsh bus depot, apart from the village of Caerau, where a few modern houses had been erected beside the country lane which then wound its way up to St Mary's church. The old church, with a history going back to the 13th century, after brave attempts at reconstruction and renewal, has been given up to the vandal, one of the darker, more mindless forces of modern society. The old lane, sadly decayed, still exists in the vicinity of the church and brings back memories of a time when, on a quiet summer evening, it could warm the heart and still the

mind to walk up the hill and across the enclosure of the fort, then down into Cwrt-yr-Ala. Following the cessation of hostilities a few 'prefabs' were erected along Caerau lane and at the foot of Sweldon hill, but they were short-lived and have been replaced by modern developments, such as Heol-yr-Odin and Lon-yr-Efail. The urbanisation of the Caerau area, with the obliteration of the old village, was the main feature of post-war council building in western Cardiff. Heol Trelai was created, linking Saintwell with the Amroth Road district and having, on its northern side, a preponderance of roads bearing topographical names, such as Tidenham Road, Bishopston Road and Haverford Way. South of Heol Trelai, in the shadow of the hill-fort, the roads are heavy with Celtic overtones and bear names like Heol-y-Berllan, Heol-y-Castell and Heol Carnau.

Except for the infilling of odd patches of ground left over from more spacious days, the growth of Ely was complete by the 'sixties and further developments were on private estates, notably in the Saintwell, St Fagans Court and Culverhouse farm areas. The latter involved the destruction of yet another charming old lane, though it could be argued in this case that it was quite inadequate to sustain the volume of traffic leaving Culverhouse Cross for St Fagans, but on the credit side educational facilities have been improved by the provision of Glan Ely, Glyn Derw and Mostyn R.C. high schools, together with supporting primary schools.

Development in the Ely area has apparently ground to a standstill at the moment, loan charges adding their weight to the campaign for conservation. Regrettably, the product of more than fifty years effort cannot be viewed with complete satisfaction, for it has not succeeded in developing a living sense of community and is already showing signs of physical decay in its older parts. A suburb must be self-renewing if it is to survive and one cannot but wonder if the Elysian fields may yet grow green again where now there is tarmac, brick and television aerial.

It's BrAIns you want!

COUNCILLOR SAMUEL ARTHUR BRAIN, writing at the turn of the century, made the proud boast that 'The Old Brewery, situate in St Mary Street, and owned by Messrs. S. A. Brain & Company, is one of the oldest establishments in Cardiff'.

Beer has been brewed at the Old Brewery in St Mary Street since 1713, although the Brain family was not involved until some considerable time later. S. A. Brain was the sole proprietor of another brewery, called the Phoenix Brewery, in Jones' Court, Womanby Street, an establishment which was sold to the Corporation in 1895, as well as being a brewer at the Old Brewery. He, together with his uncle, J. B. Brain of Clifton, purchased the Old Brewery in 1882 and the company became a limited company in 1897. The family has always been directly connected with the brewing and administration aspects of the company and currently no less than five members of the family are taking an active and major part in the conduct of the business.

The site adjacent to the Brewery and behind the *Albert Hotel* was originally known as Williams' Malt House, although all record of the malt house had disappeared by 1887, when the site was enlarged and developed with the provision of a completely new brewhouse and fermenting rooms. There has been continuous expansion throughout the decades, but due to the increasing success of traditional beer it became necessary in 1976 to redesign completely the production unit in order to increase the brewing capacity. This development has seen the boiler house moved to the extreme edge of the premises backing onto Caroline Street, while a bulk malt store is being constructed above. In due course the space made available by the removal of the old coal-fired Lancashire boilers will be filled with new fermenting rooms, racking facilities and cellarage.

The Company has its own fleet of drays to supply its customers' requirements and this fleet is constantly updated. Transport in 1917 was by steam wagon, petrol-driven wagons and horse-drawn drays. The old Yorkshire 'steamers' had horizontal boilers above the front wheels, which meant that the driver and the fireman stood in a well behind the boiler with a coal bunker between them, but the 'Thornycroft' steam wagon had a vertical boiler between the front wheels, with the driver in a well behind it and the 'steerer', as he was called, sitting on a seat on the nearside of the vehicle. This system depended for its success upon co-operation between the driver and the steerer, but when there was bad feeling between them life could be difficult.

The Company possessed the first 'Sentinel' steam wagon in Cardiff, and the makers were so proud of their machine that the Company's wagon, painted a royal blue with the name BRAINS in white letters on the front, was exhibited at one of the royal shows in Sophia Gardens. The Company had tremendous service from the Sentinel steam wagons, but the current transport is provided by diesel-driven Bedfords. A tanker has also been added to the fleet for shipping beer between the Old and the New breweries and has proved most useful during the redevelopment of the Old Brewery.

Mention should be made of the advertising slogan which has stayed with the Company for over seventy years. The idea was thought up by Mr Alfred Jones, who was a painter/signwriter with the Company and was asked to paint the Company's name over the door of a public house. This was in the year 1900 and from that time the AI has been closely associated with the Company's name. Advertising has always played a large part in sales promotion and many media have been used, from tobacco tins to television, clay pipes to newspapers, thimbles to the sides of buses. A small collection of some of these items is being preserved.

The beer brewed at the Old Brewery is of the

traditional, top-fermentation, open-fermenter, cask-conditioned variety. The dark mild is sold under the name 'Red Dragon', although it is known locally as 'Brain's Dark'. This, contrary to the national trend, is the most popular brew. The Company also brews a 'bitter', together with a 'best bitter', known as 'S.A.' which is rapidly gaining in popularity not only locally but even on a national basis, being sent as far afield as the Isle of Wight and Yorkshire when required for special occasions.

The Company owns a considerable number of public houses throughout Cardiff and district, the trading area stretching from Swansea to Bristol. Unfortunately, a lot of the older Cardiff properties are disappearing under the current redevelopment scheme, and such places as the *Empress Eugenie*,

the *Pilot*, the *Bute Road Tavern*, the *White Swan* and the *Frampton* will never be seen again. However, the Company is carrying out a continuous programme of redeveloping its houses and, during the last four years, a new house has been opened annually. It is always the intention of the Company to create atmosphere by installing or retaining some characteristic feature in a particular house, thus helping to provide a convivial meeting place for its customers.

By brewing good quality, traditional beers and supplying these throughout its trading area, the Company is endeavouring to satisfy its customers in the friendly surroundings of their own local public house, a place where they will remain convinced that 'It's Brains You Want'.

. . . wherever your thirst takes you

A familiar landmark *The Birchgrove* in Caerphilly Road. It was completely rebuilt in 1929

The *Maltsters Arms*, Merthyr Road, Whitchurch. This popular 'local' was extended in 1971

The Halfway in Cathedral Road

The ornately tiled *Golden Cross* in Custom House Street which has been scheduled as a building of special architectural and historical interest

The Westgate in Cowbridge Road East

The Heath, Whitchurch Road, will be extended during 1977/78

Neat and attractive, *The Plough* in Merthyr Road, Whitchurch. It was extended in 1962

Built to cater for the new housing estates in the area, *The Bulldog Inn*, Plasmawr Road, Fairwater, was opened in 1965

Tucked away in Old Church Road, Whitchurch, the *Fox and Hounds*, extended in 1972, remains a firm favourite with locals and visitors

These photographs of the *Maltsters Arms*, Llandaff, show (*above*) as it was before major alterations in 1964, and (*below*) as it is today

Only converted to its present use in 1974, the *Inn on the River*, situated on Taff Embankment, has already established an excellent reputation

Brain's latest house, *The Holly Bush*, built in 1977 on the Pentwyn Estate

The *Rose and Crown*, Kingsway, which was demolished in 1974; (*below*) an artist's impression of the new *Rose and Crown* which is due to be opened in 1979

An artist's impression of the extensions to the Old Brewery in St Mary Street which should be completed by 1979

The Stanley Street Murder

by John O'Sullivan

As I LEFT the *Lifeboat* hotel in Little Frederick Street, Cardiff, I paused for a while on the cobble stones of the lane dividing the public house from the neighbouring car park. This was Stanley Street, demolished in the 1930s—some 90 years after a violent death that was a landmark in the development of Cardiff, and in particular the Catholic faith in the city.

In 1848 a Welshman was stabbed to death by an Irishman in the shadow of the Catholic Church which stood on the corner of Stanley Street. It sparked off a series of incidents which can only be understood if one looks at the area as it was in the late 1840s and early 1850s.

In May 1850 Dr Thomas Webber Rammell presented a report to the General Board of Health on a preliminary inquiry into the sewerage, drainage, supply of water and the sanitary condition of the town of Cardiff. The inquiry followed a demand by one thousand petitioners for something to be done to alleviate the persistent outbreaks of cholera and typhoid common at the time.

Rammell, who blamed the high mortality rate on the recent influx of immigrants, wrote:

Nothing can be worse than the housing accommodation provided for the labouring classes and the poor in this town and the overcrowding is fearful—beyond anything of the kind I have seen . . .

Cardiff has been subjected to a greater amount of immigration than any other town of the same dimensions, and probably to a much greater proportionate amount than Liverpool itself. The immigrants consist of the most wretched members of the society from which they have been cast out—generally in starving condition, often already inflicted with disease. Of necessity, many of the immigrants will die before they have been long in the community.

Foremost among the areas condemned by Rammell was Stanley Street, lying between Bute Terrace and Lower Frederick Street, where the report of the living conditions, as supplied by Police Superintendent Stockdale, shocked even a generation aware of the more unpleasant aspects of poverty. The living room of 17 Stanley Street, visited by Stockdale in April 1849, measured 17ft 2in by 15ft 10in and was 8½ft high. It had no rear door and no windows, yet in this one unventilated room he found, eating, living and sleeping, no fewer than fifty-four men, women and children. The only furniture consisted of old orange boxes where the younger children slept to ensure that they were not crushed during the night. The stinking, unwashed, ragged inhabitants had with them their few, paltry possessions, including salt fish, heaps of rags, bones and rotten potatoes. They shared an uncovered privy which was full to overflowing, flooding the outside yard with sewage. Outside, the dark alleyway that was Stanley Street was littered with offensive decaying vegetable matter and other refuse dumped there by the inhabitants.

Most houses were rented at four shillings a week and filled with lodgers who payed threepence a night (half-price for children) for the doubtful privilege of having one of these roofs over their heads. Four or five families lived in most houses in Stanley Street and the neighbouring Mary Ann Street. In one dwelling, where the privy was under the stairs, the hole was covered by a stone at night to provide a pillow for one more head. Under these conditions it was no surprise that the cholera outbreak of 1848 claimed nineteen lives in Stanley Street alone, with another sixteen in David Street and twelve in Mary Ann Street.

In spite of their horrific living conditions (perhaps even helped by common adversity) the Irish clung together, pinning their faith and hopes for this world and the next on their Catholic religion. Before the Irish influx the Catholic church in Britain consisted, according to Cardinal Newman, of '. . . a mere handful of individuals, found in corners, alleys and cellars . . .'

In 1820 there were only three catholics in Cardiff. They were joined by a group of six Irishmen, including John Driscoll, who, in the latter part of the century, lived with his daughter in Bedford Place, Cardiff. It was Driscoll who related to Fr. Fortunato Signini an interesting story which typifies the Welsh attitude of the time to Catholicism.

Fr. Signini, whose diary of his stay in Cardiff is still at St Peter's rectory, wrote a letter shortly before his death in 1889 in which he tells how, according to Driscoll, a handful of Catholics would go to Newport or Merthyr Tydfil at least once a month to hear Sunday Mass. It was then decided to invite a Fr. Portle, an Irish priest, to travel from Merthyr to Cardiff to conduct a service. News of the visit spread and a Welshman asked Driscoll if it was right that a Roman priest was to conduct a service in Cardiff. 'Quite true', was the reply, 'and what have you to say against it?'. 'Why, nothing', said the Welshman, 'but I would very much like to see him. Will you show him to me?' The Welshman then proceeded to offer Driscoll half-a-crown to point out the visiting priest. Driscoll readily accepted, but, as he pointed out Fr. Portal stepping from the coach, the Welshman gasped, 'He is nothing but a gentleman—and a fine gentleman, too!' Fr. Signini, writing more than sixty years later, made the wry comment that the Welshman fully expected that the priest would resemble 'that awful creature who is often painted with two horns, flaming eyes, tremendously sharp nails and even cloven feet'.

That first Mass was said at the home of John Donohue at 21 Union Street, the site of which is close to the present cathedral in Charles Street, Cardiff. As the small band of Catholics grew in number Sunday Mass became a regular feature and was celebrated at a variety of places, including the *Red Lion*, the *Nicholls Arms*, Bute Street, and a warehouse at the rear of the Customs House. The altar boys learned the Latin necessary to serve the priests from a hunchbacked Irish Protestant schoolmaster by the name of Morgan.

The Relief Act of 1829 emancipated the Catholics of Britain and by 1840 there were a thousand practising the faith in Cardiff, when the first resident priest, Fr. Dwyer, was appointed. Attempts were made to purchase a plot of land in Charles Street to build a church, but the fashionable residents objected to the 'poor worshippers' invading their exclusive area. Then one James Stivarenghi secured a piece of ground at the rear of David Street from a builder named John Highwall and Fr. Patrick Millea set to and built the first Catholic church in the growing town of Cardiff. But the progress of Roman Catholicism was not smooth and was soon to be violently interrupted.

On the evening of 11 November 1848, John Richards was returning from a wake at a house in Love Lane. As he walked home he was joined by Thomas Lewis and his wife, who was carrying a baby in her arms. Lewis was 30 years of age, a collier, and the son of the landlord of the *Red Lion Hotel*. He lived with his wife and three children in an overcrowded terraced house in David Street. The party called at the *Pembroke Castle Hotel* and then headed for David Street. As they reached the top of Stanley Street they heard a noise near the Catholic church. Thomas Lewis went to investigate and got into an argument with John Connors, an Irishman who was unknown to him. As Lewis walked back to his wife Connors hurled a stone and hit the Welshman on the back of his legs, causing Mrs Lewis to drop her baby in fright. Connors then ran after Lewis and stabbed him four times with a knife which he used for eating. Lewis died almost immediately.

Superintendent Jeremiah Box Stockdale, head of the twelve-man Cardiff police force, was on duty near Hayes Bridge and was congratulating himself on the peaceful night he was enjoying when the stillness was broken by the sound of running footsteps and the piercing scream of a terrified woman. On investigating, he went to Stanley Street and found that the body of the murdered man had been taken home and placed in a chair. Stockdale had no trouble in getting a description of the wanted killer, but Connors had vanished.

The first hint of trouble between the Welsh and Irish came the next morning when policemen walked into the Catholic church during Mass and removed John Cokely, an Irish labourer who was known to have been at the scene of the murder. He denied any knowledge of the incident, but later, at the inquest, admitted that he had actually shared a bed with Connors after the killing and that the wanted Irishman had remained hidden in the Cokely house, 17 Mary Anne Street, for at least twenty-four hours. The non-co-operation continued when Stockdale was informed that three Irishmen, including Connors, had taken a boat for Cork that morning, though this turned out to be false information. Cokely stubbornly refused to answer questions, only replying with a piece of proverbial wisdom, 'A man who puts his hands in his pocket and keeps his tongue between his teeth is safe'.

On the Monday morning the murder was formally reported to the Mayor, Walter Coffin, and a jury was impanelled to view the body at the home of the widow. It was reported by the *Cardiff and Merthyr Guardian* that the dead man 'looked calm' but had a vicious gash on his left cheek. The weeping widow insisted that her husband was

The *Red Lion* on the corner of Kingsway and Queen Street, one of the places where Catholic Mass was first celebrated
Photograph courtesy Western Mail & Echo Ltd

not drunk when he met Connors, but had died because he had remonstrated with the Irishman for throwing stones at them, while John Richards told the coroner that he had seen little of the incident as it was always dark in Stanley Street, even when the moon was shining, for the Catholic church threw big shadows across the narrow road which divided the two rows of houses.

The Lewis murder was the last straw for the Welsh. Earlier in the year two more Irish immigrants had had their death sentences commuted after the murders of two Welshmen. An infuriated crowd, estimated at hundreds, stormed through the area seeking revenge for the murder and for the aid given to the killer of one of their countrymen, but also seeking for the killer himself. No house was safe. The chanting crowd, armed with stones from three cartloads of pitching material which had been conveniently placed in the road, demanded that the Catholic chapel and the priest's house should be searched. The doors were forced and the premises searched, but without result. The *Cardiff and Merthyr Guardian* of 18 November excelled itself with sensational headlines.

DREADFUL RIOT IN CARDIFF: THE MILITARY CALLED OUT: HORRIBLE STATE OF EXCITEMENT: FURIOUS ATTACK OF THE WELSH UPON THE IRISH: FLIGHT OF THE CATHOLIC PRIEST: DEMOLITION OF CATHOLIC CHAPEL AND PRIEST'S RESIDENCE: TWO HOUSES BURNT: INTENSE EXCITEMENT OF THE PEOPLE AND VERDICT OF THE JURY.

The start of the report read: 'These and other rumours were about in Cardiff today . . .' In spite of the lurid headlines, the total damage was no more than six pounds. Some windows were smashed and the parish priest, F. Millea, considerably frightened, escaped into the crowd, assisted by a friend, Mrs Hannah Hemmingway, and a suitable disguise. (The Hemmingways lived in a big house at Plwcca Lane, later known as Castle Road, now City Road. The building, which jutted out into the highway, causing a bottle-

neck, was demolished in the early 1890s. A dairy now stands on the site, which is at the corner of St Peter's Street and City Road). Fr. Millea was accused by the *Guardian* of deserting his post when he should have stayed with his flock.

News of the Cardiff troubles spread quickly. The driver of the mail coach told the people of Chepstow that the town was under siege. The Mayor had handbills printed calling for peace and calm, the military were standing by, and, the ultimate deterrent, twenty tradesmen, armed with staves made by sawing in half ten mop handles, were sworn in as special constables.

The hunt for Connors continued without success. The *Guardian* (18 December) carried an offer of a fifty pounds reward for the capture of the wanted man. The advertisement, by Superintendent Stockdale, makes interesting reading for journalists who are shackled by reporting restrictions in the progressive 1970s.

£50 Reward. John Connors (or Connor) an Irishman is charged with the murder of Thomas Lewis on Saturday, November 11, in Stanley Street, Cardiff. The said John Connors is said to be about 27 or 30 years of age, of dark complexion, dark hair and whiskers which are rather large, and was dressed in a white round moleskin jacket with pearl buttons, dark trousers, and wore a blue cloth cap with peak, but sometimes wears a white Billy cock hat. His height is about 5ft 9ins or 10ins. He is supposed to have a slight mark or bend on the nose. He is a navigator and will most probably seek employment on a railway.

The day of the funeral brought further headaches for Stockdale. One hundred and fifty Irish navvies, employed in building the South Wales Railway, fearful for the safety of their fellow countrymen and particularly their priest, marched into the town, armed with shovels and pick-axes. They formed a menacing crowd along the route as the funeral procession wound its way to St John's cemetery in Adamsdown. After the funeral they marched on the police station in St Mary Street and demanded that the parish pay for the repairs to the church and the presbytery. The demand was met.

While Stockdale was busy keeping the peace in Cardiff, investigations continued in the valley towns to the north of the port. Superintendent Thomas, a fluent Welsh speaker, moved about the navvy camps seeking information. He also set two men, watched by a third, to walk the railway track from Newbridge (now known as Pontypridd) to Bridgend. His inquiries led to raids on a number of houses in the Newbridge area. As he shone his lantern on a bed in a lodging house a man sat up and said, 'Do you suspect me? If you do you had better take me'. The man gave his name as James Gogan, but, acting on a hunch, Thomas took him to Cardiff, where he was positively identified as the wanted killer, Connors.

The inquest was resumed at the old courthouse in St Mary Street and the jury wasted little time in bringing in a verdict of 'Wilful murder' against the Irishman, who claimed that he had not left Cardiff until seven days after the murder of Lewis. The streets of the town were lined with jeering Welshmen as Connors was taken by horse-drawn fly to the county gaol.

The trial by newspaper continued, despite the fact that the Irishman was committed for trial at the Assizes and, therefore, stood in the shadow of the gallows. The *Cardiff and Merthyr Guardian* went so far as to report unconfirmed stories that Connors had murdered a man in Ireland and had also viciously assaulted another person in Cardiff, while the paper demanded, in righteous indignation, to know how Connors had managed to

Old St David's Catholic Church photographed in 1970 with Stanley Street name plate on the side. This was the scene of the killing
Photograph courtesy Cardiff Central Library

remain concealed in Cardiff for at least twenty-four hours and possibly as much as seven days, living in the immediate vicinity of the incident. The Rammell report, with its revelations of hideous overcrowding, inclines the modern reader to sympathise with the difficulties facing Stockdale.

The Assizes opened with much pomp at Swansea on 27 February 1849, after a dinner at the *Mackworth Arms*. The Assize judge, Sir William Erle attended Divine Service at St Mary's Church the following day, where the text for the sermon was, 'Wherefore ye must needs be subject only for wrath, but also for conscience sake'. On the Monday the lists of cases was a formidable one, including three cases of wounding by stabbing, one of shooting, two of rape, and the murder charge against John Connors. The case for the prosecution against the latter was presented by Benjamin Matthews, attorney. Connors was not represented and pleaded not guilty. The evidence was very much as given at the inquest, except that Connors, by examining witnesses, sought to establish that he had only stabbed Lewis after the latter had seized him by the neckerchief. After the prosecution had presented its case, Connors said, 'I am a poor man and have no friends to give me a character'. In his summing-up the judge stressed that the jury must be satisfied that Connors intended to kill Lewis before they could find him guilty of murder and, in the event, a verdict of 'Manslaughter' was returned.

Addressing the guilty man the judge said, 'John Connors, you stand convicted of the crime of manslaughter after a very careful and anxious consideration on the part of the jury in which they have deliberated long whether or not your crime did not amount to murder . . .' He expressed himself satisfied with the verdict, though the crime in his opinion approached very closely to murder, and Connors was sentenced to be 'transported beyond the seas' for the remainder of his natural life.

The episode of the Stanley Street murder thus ended with Connors being shipped off to Botany Bay in the hold of a convict ship, Fr. Patrick Millea transferred from the Cardiff mission at his own request, and the widow Lewis and her children saved from the workhouse by the proceeds of a public appeal, to which even the inquest jurymen contributed their fees. Out of the tragic events of that night in November, 1848, came some good, for the national publicity given to the incident and to the Rammell report brought Stanley Street and the neighbouring area to the attention of the Catholic church authorities. In 1854 Fr. Signini was appointed to the mission and left his mark in more than forty years of devoted service.

Fr. Signini was responsible for the erection of the old St David's school, now closed, which was built on a site adjacent to the Stanley Street Chapel. The foundation stone was blessed on 17 October 1855, when offerings totalling thirty pounds were placed on the slab. When the school, which in 1977 was being used as a youth centre and council offices, was opened on 1 September 1856, it catered for 150 boys, 130 girls and 120 infants. By 1859 the Catholic population of Cardiff had grown to 10,000, while by 1977 there were more than twenty churches and as many schools catering for a Catholic population of more than 30,000.

In the Ecumenical atmosphere created by the Vatican II Council, Christian unity is much in evidence in the city, a unity of which Fr. Signini was an early supporter. In his letter of 1889, four decades after the Stanley Street murder, he made it clear that the ignorance and suspicion that led to the story of the Welshman and the half-crown belonged to the past. The letter continues:

Let us thank God for the change, and that now, as I was happy to find in my own time at Cardiff, Catholics, Anglicans and Dissenters can meet in good fellowship and respect another's honest religious convictions and join in much that is good. May this be a prelude to that blessed consummation to which so many are anxiously looking forward when it is said that there is but one Fold and One Shepherd.

The author wishes to acknowledge the assistance he has received from Mr. G. A. C. Dart, Librarian of South Glamorgan, and his staff at the Reference Department, Cardiff Central Library.

Down Memory Lane

'Read all about it—Cardiff a City'. Monday 23 October 1905—Cardiff is elevated to the status of a city but today it is the youthful *Echo* seller who catches the eye in this fascinating Fletcher study

Illustrations in this section are reproduced by courtesy of Cardiff Central Library

The old Taff Vale Railway Bridge in Queen Street decorated for the visit of the Lord Mayor of London (Sir David Evans) in 1892

University College students answering their country's call in the First World War

A busy corner of Cardiff Market on a Saturday in the early 1900s. Michael Marks (of Marks and Spencer fame) started trading there in 1895

The excitement is clearly evident in this 'day after' the Relief of Mafeking photograph taken on 18 May 1900. Readers will recognise the location as the corner of St Mary Street and Mill Lane

The last private houses in Queen Street between Windsor Place and Dumfries Place being demolished in 1925

St John's National School. This building stood across and at right angles to what is now the Friary. The photograph was taken prior to demolition *c*.1912

Church Street and The Hayes are immediately recognisable in these views taken by Ernest T. Bush in the early 1920s

COMPLETION OF THE BUTE EAST DOCK, CARDIFF.

THE extension of this stupendous work was completed on the 1st of September, and Wednesday, the 14th ult., was fixed upon as the day of opening. Preparations on an extensive scale had been made for the due celebration of an event of so much importance to the town and port of Cardiff; but, owing to the sudden death of Lord James Stuart—who for many years had represented the boroughs of Cardiff, Cowbridge, and Llantrisant in Parliament, and who was the maternal uncle of the young Marquis of Bute, under whose auspices the opening of the dock was to be inaugurated—the intended festivities were dispensed with, and the dock was opened for trade in the quietest possible manner.

We extract from the *Cardiff and Merthyr Guardian* some particulars of the opening ceremony, and of the capacity of the dock :—"The formal opening took place on Wednesday, the 14th ult. About twelve o'clock the Marquis, accompanied by his trustees, the Right Honourable James Stuart

Wortley, and John Boyle, Esq.; Miss Boyle, Miss E. Boyle; and Mr. C. his Lordship's tutor, arrived at the dock in the Marchioness's p carriage, and proceeded to the office of the resident engineer, M'Connochie, situated on the west quay, where, boats being in readiness, embarked for the *United States* steamer, the property of the Bute Steam Towing Company, which was lying on the east side, ready to tow the Extension the British barque *Masaniello*, which had just ar to take in a cargo of coals. After a pleasant ride across the boats the select party boarded the *United States*, where a limited nu of gentlemen interested in the success of the undertaking awaiting their arrival. Steam being up, the *United States* commenced peaceful errand of conducting the *Masaniello* into the Extension, amid hearty cheers of those on board, and of taking her round to the west where she was moored to discharge her ballast. The *United States* proceeded with her distinguished party down to the dock gates, and a wards returned to the top of the dock, where the Marquis and his p

The opening of the Bute East Dock, as reported in *The Illustrated London News* 1 October 1859

ST DOCK CARDIFF.

barked and entered the family carriage amid the enthusiastic cheers few who, having heard of the intended formal opening, had hastened spot. At the same time as the dock was entered by the *United States* *Masaniello*, the new canal, which forms a junction with the Bute West and the Glamorgan Ship Canal, was opened by one of the Aberdare Company's boats (No. 267), with a cargo of coal for Messrs. David and and an empty lighter, passing through the locks. With the exception small steamer belonging to the contractors for the works, Messrs. ngway and Co., which followed the *Masaniello* with a small party, this uted the whole of the opening of the extension.

he Bute East Dock was commenced early in 1852, the trustees at the time the much-lamented Mr. Tyndall Bruce and Mr. Macnabb, and the ers Sir John Rennie and Mr. John Plews. The first portion—in 1000 feet, and width 300 feet—was opened in July, 1855. The first ion, 2000 feet in length and 500 wide, was commenced early in 1855 s. Walker, Burgess, and Cooper being the engineers), and was opened

in 1857. The second and last extension, of 1300 feet by 500, was begun by the same engineers in 1857, and completed on the 1st of September last, including a junction canal communicating with the Bute West Dock and the Glamorgan Canal. The whole of the works have been executed by Messrs. Hemingway and Co. The water area of this dock alone is 45 acres, and the basin $2\frac{1}{4}$ acres; height of sill of sea-gates at springs, 31 feet $8\frac{1}{2}$ inches; height at neaps, 21 feet $7\frac{1}{2}$ inches; sea-gates, width, 55 feet; sea-lock, length between gates, 220 feet—width, 55 feet; inner lock, length between gates, 220 feet—width, 50 feet. The depth of water throughout the dock is 25 feet. The Bute East Dock is thus capable of accommodating the largest ships in the merchant service. Fifteen coal-staiths are already erected, and it is intended to put up seven more, which will give, when complete, a shipping power in this dock alone of a million tons and a half of coal per year."

The accommodation for shipping in the port of Cardiff is very great, there being, besides the Bute East Dock above described, the Bute West Dock, the Bute Tidal Dock, and the Glamorgan Ship Canal.

A stroll in the park was a pleasure to be savoured in the early years of this century. The swings in Thompson's Park *(above)* were a great attraction, while *(below)* the bandstand was the magnet at Roath Park

'Votes for Women'. A deputation of suffragettes leaves Cardiff for London to meet Mr Asquith, *(inset)* Mrs Keating Hill addresses porters and cabmen; *(below)* suffragettes outside Cardiff City Hall at the start of a 'grand march' on 15 June 1908

Temperance Town, c.1930. So called because of a stipulation by the land-owner that no public house should be erected in this area of small houses and narrow streets which was located north of the General Railway Station on the site now occupied by the Central Bus Station

A. E. Jones's butchers' shop in System Street, Adamsdown, Christmas 1891

This was the forerunner of the 'pink paraffin man' touring the streets of Cardiff at the end of the last century selling 'burning oil' to householders. The photograph was taken in Tyler Street, Roath, c.1895

117

A relatively traffic-free Cowbridge Road, Canton, *c*.1920